Playing A Your GAME

Stay Motivated, Remain Focused and Succeed in School and Life

Kantis Simmons

To: _____

From: _____

Only one game in life counts, and that's Your "A" Game

Playing Your A Game

ISBN 978-0-9767812-1-9

Simmons, Kantis
Playing Your "A" Game:
Stay Motivated, Remain Focused, and Succeed in School & Life

Copyright 2011 by The SIMAKAN Group, Atlanta, Georgia

Artwork/Design: Christina Jones, FlyMajorLifestyle.com
Photography: Wendy Jenkins

Printed and bound in the United States of America

For additional information on Kantis Simmons, please visit
www.KantisSimmons.com

I dedicate this book to everyone that has sown into my life.

I also dedicate this book to everyone that has sown into your life.

It's because of the people in our lives, that we are who we are today.

May they reap greatly from the seeds they have sown.

"An applicable…informative…and easy to understand system that impacts both the personal and academic aspects of life."
– Dr. Tanea Chane (Pharmacy Graduate), Minneapolis, MN

"Playing Your "A" Game is a practical tool that keeps me on track. It keeps me organized, prepared, and on top of my game. Plus, It encourages me not to give up, and that I really can do all things…including acing Organic Chemistry, mastering Cell biology, managing work and social activities!"
- Aprielle Brakley, Hampton University, VA

" I found your book to be very educationally and naturally uplifting, I really enjoyed reading it. The chapter on discipline, consistency, and diligence really stands out for me, as well as, taking confidence into my studies. I have been changed."

- Mechel Desears, University of Georgia, Athens, GA

CONTENTS

introduction

School Days

Imagine this...

There are only 7 seconds left on the clock in the fourth quarter of the NBA basketball finals; our team is down by two points, and the next basket will determine if we are the World Basketball Champions or not.

What player in the NBA would you want to give the ball to, to shoot the game winning shot? What athlete actually comes to your mind?

It's the 18th hole of the PGA Golf Tournament, and your very next putt will win you 2 million dollars. What pro golfer do you think about?

Let's say you are participating in the Australian open or Wimbledon tennis tournament and your excellent play results in you being the #1 tennis player in the world. What professional tennis player do you think about?

In all of these cases, I personally think of people like Kobe Bryant, Michael Jordan, Lebron James. Golfers like Tiger Woods and Phil Mickelson. Tennis players like Venus and Serena Williams, Andre Agassi and Roger Federer. Each of these athletes are known for being the top players in their sport. They consistently play their "A" Game, and put their best foot forward to win and excel, and it was demonstrated in every one of their championship events.

Professional athletes recognize the importance of being at their best. They realize that their individual performances have a direct impact on their team and organization. If they are at their finest or playing their "A" Game, competitors and observers will notice. It is at these times that they seem unstoppable. This peak performing zone can also be experienced in other areas of life; in business, in relationships, in finances, and especially in academics.

I get it.

I understand.

I feel your pain.

I know your struggles.

I hear your requests.

I have failed.

I have won.

I have failed again.

I have gotten up, and won again.

I have done it.

I have done it all, (mostly all).

And you will too.

You Got Game

All students desire to be at the top; however, their work habits and levels of discipline do not always support their scholastic desires. What is it that causes one student to perform poorly and another to play his or her "A" Game all year long? This book answers that question.

In Playing Your "A" Game - Stay Motivated, Remain Focused, and Succeed in School & Life I will share my best kept secrets, my most embarrassing failures, and all the tested proven ideas I've learned during 25 years of being in school, after receiving 3 college degrees with honors and more than a decade of working with students, schools and educators.

I've spent five years in preschool, seven years in elementary school, five years in high school, four years in college, and four more years as a graduate student; that's 25 years of school experience. Now don't be misled to think that I experienced automatic success with a transcript full of A's. This was not the case, but when I consistently learned and applied the key strategies of learning, I tapped into a level of educational success that consistently brought promotion and favor.

Now why after all this time am I putting all this information in one resource?

It's very simple, look at these disappointing numbers.

7,000 students drop out every single school day.

1.3 million students fail to graduate from high school every year.

Only 1 in 3 college freshman will graduate and get a job in their field.

I'm tired of reading numbers like this. It absolutely grieves me.

Plus, I'm tired of seeing good students make bad mistakes, trapped by negative thoughts which result in a life of always under achieving.

I'm also committed to answering the questions of parents on how to get the best out of their kids, especially after hearing their many frustrations and complaints on *how my child won't... my child does this... I'm wasting money on this... and my child's teacher tells me this.*

Plus this is my contribution to assist and serve the many superintendents, presidents, deans, principals, educators, professors, teachers, counselors, coaches, directors, youth workers, and administrators. I choose to help them do what they consistently do all year long to produce better students, better schools, better communities and a better world.

Lastly, this edition of Playing Your "A" Game is written so many won't have to repeat the frustrations, negative attitudes, procrastinations, and setbacks that I eventully overcame from grade school to grad school.

Like the time when I almost didn't graduate from high school even though I had the highest G.P.A. in my high school, because I was too lazy to read in Sr. Literature.

Or when I was disappointed to hear that I lost a full academic band scholarship to the first school of my choice because I came up 40 points short on the SAT Reasoning Test (actually my mindset was the reason I kept scoring low on that test).

And when I was so stressed and so exhausted that I fell asleep while ironing my shirt before a very important presentation for some corporate sponsors while in grad school. (Yikes! I was super late to my presentation with red eyes, a wrinkled shirt, and a terrible demonstration. All due to procrastination.)

Whether you are a student looking to get better grades, stay motivated, remain focused, or you are an educator who's looking for ways to increase morale and performance of your students in school. Whether you are parent who wants to end the frustration of your child under achieving and you're lost for answers - this is for you.

You Can Win, If You Will
I would love to guarantee that this book alone will help you get a transcript full of A's, an academic career of undefeated victories, and a life free from failures. But this is just a book, a good book that is. A book of pages that is NOTHING, if you don't take action.

Just as a football team uses a playbook to outmaneuver its opponents during a game, this book will share with you 7.25 foundational principles for academic success. These 'plays' will open your eyes to a new way of approaching school matters. Specifically, it will show you how to:

• Get and stay motivated when you dread studying or going to school.

• Overcome procrastination and get things done quicker.

• Set academic goals and accomplish every one of them.

• Balance school, family and social time to be more productive.

• Increase your classroom confidence and defeat test anxiety.

• Increase your focus while preventing distractions that throw your day off.

• Create positive habits that will help get you better grades.

• And a few statements on how to land school scholarships.

Hi, I'm Kantis...

Now before I dive in with all the contents of this book, I learned from my good friend Jonathan Sprinkles, that people won't hear you, unless they know you. So for you to better understand who I am as an author, you first must understand me as a person.

Now I was raised in a middle class broke family in Atlanta, Georgia. If you know about being middle class broke, you will understand that my great parents raised me very well, but we were financially broke (at least that's what it appeared to me growing up).

Middle class broke is where you have both the mother and the father in the home married, both people working and you're always broke. Middle class broke is when you have a nice house with nice green grass but you're always broke. Middle class broke is when you can only take vacations on the weekend because someone had to always be working throughout the weekday.

In spite of this financial status, my mom and dad did a great job of keeping me busy, and a great job of teaching me that I can do anything that I wanted to do. At times I felt they were only doing this because they wanted to make sure that I was raised in a nurtured environment after the troubled birth I had, which later lead to years of insecurity and acceptance issues.

Even though money was not always flowing through

the bank accounts like we were the Cosby's; my parents knew how to make ends meet. I've always had a meal on the table and I've always been trained to walk in excellence,taught to be honest, and work hard.

As a child I was constantly engaged in doing something; whether it was playing baseball, singing in the church choir, playing in the band, running a lawn business, selling Mary Kay or doing my household chores.

"LOL! Did i just say Mary Kay Cosmetics?" (too funny)

My mom actually believes and preaches to this day, *"If you are not busy doing something positive, you will find yourself busy doing something negative"*.

Due to the fact that my parents were readers, leaders, feeders, and breeders they passed down their educational genes and taught me principles like:

• Don't quit!

• Become self-sufficient, and learn to work with others.

• Think before you act.

• It's okay to mess up, just get up, learn from your mistakes, and strive for your best.

• You can do anything in life, if you will.

• Use your head for more than a hat rack. Think!

• You can be and have anything you want.

• Quit crying, before I give you something to cry about. LOL!

• Trust God and trust yourself.

• Be up front with people and communicate.

• Always be honest and tell the truth.

• Look into the future, predict it and be two steps ahead.

Growing up as a child, both of my parents had to work so that meant my mom immediately rolled me into my very first school at the age of 6 weeks. I was enrolled at Young World Nursery in Decatur, Georgia.

I crawled those nursery walls until the age of 6. I vaguely remember a few of my classmates and teachers, however I fully remember the many graduations and commencement services I had. Seems as if we held a graduation ceremony every year and we wore the white cap and gown with the blue graduation tassels, with the little dangling year on it.

As I think about it, those graduation ceremonies marked me as a person. So when I see anyone graduate from school I feel the warm and fuzzies on the inside.

The Bow and the Panther

After my 5 years at Young World, I transitioned to Rainbow Elementary and spent 7 glorious years in that school. It's amazing that after all the decades that have passed by, I still communicate and stay in contact with many of my Rainbow Crew. Thank you Facebook.

Rainbow was my development years. It was the years that I realized I was different. It was the years where I was picked on; it was the years where I wanted to be accepted. It was the years where I was trying to keep up. It was the years where I was short. It was the years I battled with reading comprehension.

I was a fast reader, and proud of it, but I didn't do a good job of comprehending what I read. Because of this, I didn't like the "reading" classes. Classes like English, Social Studies and History, but was drawn to classes like math, science, P.E., I loved to figure stuff out. After my development days under the Bow, middle school was not an option for me; because my elementary school was one of the feeder schools for my high school and it actually sat across the street from Rainbow.

I entered high school at 8th grade. My oh my, High School was like a Heaven, it seemed so big and it was so indescribable. Students were bigger, the classes were bigger. The upper class girls looked like grown women, and the athletes were big and buff. This was Southwest DeKalb High School in Decatur, Georgia, the home of the Panthers.

This high school was the pride and joy of the community, and it was also the most hated by the other city schools - because athletically we ranked tops in the major sports like football, basketball, baseball and track. School pride was at an all-time high. We too had a great marching band and our academics were superb.

High school is where I learned excellence. It was here, where I was exposed to great opportunities. It was here, where I found my self excelling in the sciences and math. It was here, where my reading comprehension got better. It was here, where I learned leadership.

At the end of my sophomore year in high school, I was selected to be the Head Drum Major of the Marching Band. Oh boy, my life changed. That position taught me discipline, time management and life management as a student.

Along with managing schoolwork and band work, I had baseball work, church work, choir work, grass work, and house work; which all taught me priorities. Not only that, it taught me the importance of an hour.

If you focus for 60 minutes there is a lot you can make happen within that time frame. Life management was

23

essential to my academic and student success. As you will see in this book, it has to be for you too.

Graduating from high school was a challenge, because the second semester of my senior year I was unmotivated in my A.P. English/Literature class. My grades dropped, I didn't fully prepare for tests, and didn't put the time and effort in to fully reading my books and doing my assignments. I was about to graduate, right?

Even though my G.P.A. was the highest for any male at Southwest Dekalb, and I was termed Mr. Panther for this accomplishment, I almost didn't graduate because I had a failing grade in my A.P. English class. With only a few weeks left till graduation my English teacher pulled me aside, called my mother and told me of the bad news. "if you don't pass this class you will not be able to graduate, nor complete the required high school curriculum."

OH BOY!

So you know how the story ended, I got my grades up. I did extra credit work, I spent time in my teacher's office, I absolutely grinded my way to a "C" out of that course. And because it was an Advanced Placement course, I was actually credited the value of a "B" on my transcript.

Learn from me - it's better to start strong, stay strong and finish stronger in each and every one of your classes. At the same time this was going on, I was in the middle of the college search process and locating scholarships and money for school.

My school counselors were very aggressive in preparing me and my senior class for the next level. They kept the right information before our eyes, they offered us inside advise. They wrote recommendations, and they even made phone calls. Because of them, my parents, and my keen sense to apply for EVERY scholarship that crossed my desk, I had scholarship offers in baseball, science, band, and academics. However, none of them was for the full amount, except to some of the small schools that I didn't want to attend.

We're Still Middle Class Broke

Out of all the scholarship offers that I received, there was one school that I really wanted to go to, and that was Florida A&M University in Tallahassee, Florida. I wanted to attend there because they had a great Science and Engineering program, they were only 5 hours away from home, and because they had an awesome band program. They were the world renowned "Marching 100".

I was offered a full academic band scholarship with FAMU (as they are also known). After my great interview with their band, visiting there school and the band program, having a music audition, receiving the bells and whistles about their school, they finally agreed to offer me a full academic band scholarship. I was so geeked, because I wanted to be the first dark-skinned short Head Drum Major to lead that Marching Band on the field. All I had to do was, submit my S.A.T. scores.

I Hate the S.A.T.

Opps, I forgot to tell you, I hated taking standardized tests. Like most students, I would clam up.

I would over think. I would have sweaty palms. I would toss and turn the nights before the test. I would be a nervous wreck whenever a standardized test would come up. Why? Because I hated the reading comprehension parts on the test. To my disappointment after taking the SAT four times, I came up 40 points short of the minimum requirement that Florida A&M needed to give me the full academic band scholarship.

Yikes! They took the scholarship offer away, ripped my agreement letter and told me "Sorry Kantis".

Devastated! Devastated! Devastated! I was completely hurt and torn up.

I knew that my middle class broke family didn't have the money to pay for my full college education. I didn't want a school loan with four years of financial debt. I was the highest GPA'd student in my class. Heck, I was "Kantis Simmons" (in a prideful tone).

Because of the entrepreneurial spirit that I received from my dad, I did have a lawn service business from the age of eight. On that Saturday after hearing the terrible news, I was cutting my favorite clients yard - Mrs. Gardner.

As I followed the cutting lines, I paced back and forth with the lawn mower in front of me, I thought about my disappointing future and tears began to roll down my face, and I started crying like a baby - all while cutting the yard.

Mrs. Gardner noticed that her lawn guy was weeping, so she runs outside and says to me, "Kantis, what is wrong with you? Why are you crying?"

I proceeded to mumble the reasons out while sounding like a 4 year old who's crying and trying to explain to his mom why he wanted the toy out of the store that he couldn't get and is now whining.

After 3 attempts to clearly communicate my hurt and pain, I told her that I would be cutting her grass all my life, because my parents didn't have enough money to pay my way to college.

She listened, she hugged me, and she told me to "Never Quit". She informed me about a school in Virginia that had an awesome science honors program, and gave me the details on who to call and when to call.

She knew this program perfectly, because her daughter was a graduating senior in the program and headed to medical school. Norfolk State University - DNIMAS Program was my answer. I did as she instructed.

27

I called the appropriate gentleman. I marketed myself as instructed, and I showed them that I was a *'sexy student'*.

Here's a Great Note on Scholarships

Note => To receive any scholarship as a student, you must look *sexy* on paper; meaning your academic transcript must show and demonstrate that you can do the work. Colleges feel that if you have excelled in the past, then you should be able to excel in the future. What you do outside of the classroom is just as important as what you do inside of the classroom.

Just like people don't like to buy ugly cars or trucks, colleges don't like to invest scholarship money in *ugly* students. The 3 step key to get scholarships is this:

Show Yourself - apply for the money.
Market Yourself - advertise your strengths.
Sell Yourself - amplify who you are.

After receiving this full academic scholarship to Norfolk State University and finishing a degree in Chemistry I went on to receive a full graduate school fellowship that paid my way through grad school as I completed two Masters Degrees from Lehigh University and Georgia Tech.

With all that education, I spent 10 years of my life working as a research scientist for NASA Research Center, and for CIBA vision where I developed new contact lens products.

Let me stop here. Let me stop sharing my academic journey all in one chapter. Since this is my book, I can spread the story out over many pages, right?

This book is my way of passing down truths, advice, and strategies on school and life success. The things that I will share, were not only learned from my parents, but things that I have learned from my friends, my teachers and professors, my closest friends, my mentors, from the smart people's books I have read, from employers, from colleagues, from great TV shows, from my Pastors, from the Bible, from the dictionary and from every day-to-day experience I have learned over these few decades.

I've arranged this book as an Academic Playbook. You can jump from chapter to chapter if you desire, or read the book all the way straight through. All that I ask is that you take massive action.

I will share the principles, the academic secrets, the advise and the learning points - but remember, you must apply ACTION to win this game.

Let's Play Your "A" Game.

play #1

Have a Pep Rally

Students mimic this behavior, and teachers are looking for ways to solve it...

> *"I would like to know how to get my daughter motivated for school when she has absolutely no interest. She is 17 and will not be graduating next year due to her marks. She just doesn't seem to care. If the course subject does not come easy to her, she just won't do it. She doesn't put in any extra effort. If it's not something that can be done in class, she just won't do it. She has never brought homework home for years and it had finally all caught up to her last year. She is now trying to play catchup but not succeeding. When she does put forth an effort, she can get very good marks but she is just lazy and unmotivated when it comes to school. I don't know what else to try,"*

Does this sound familiar? Do you see parts of your self in this mother's confession?

I realize their are times during your academic career where it can become difficult to stay motivated and avoid burnout, especially when school is 9 months of the year.

School Sucks, Kinda

As a student, you must learn not only how to become effective with student skills, but also how to manage frustration, and at times, the feeling that you lack the necessary motivation to move forward. There are several things you can do to remain motivated and focused on what it takes to progress through your program and earn your diploma and/or degree.

It's my highest opinion and belief that the main reason students don't do good in school is because of a lack of motivation. Studies have shown and I'm sure you agree that the classes and courses you are most motivated about are the classes and courses you get the best grades in.

Getting through school requires more than hard work, it takes mastery of educational skills and a perseverance to press during seasons of challenge.

Whenever a baseball player hits a batting slump, or a basketball player hits a shooting slump, they are consistently taught to stay with the fundamentals and keep performing.

The tools, tips, techniques, ideas and advice in this book is geared to help you incorporate the right skills into your everyday life and make it easier to become a successful student. Staying motivated in schoolwork requires encouragement and help.

So let me help you, lets talk about the opposite of being motivated - and that's apathy.

Apathy is a state of indifference, or the suppression of emotions such as concern, excitement, motivation and passion.

A few Indicators of Apathy

• Your academic gas tank is running empty, and you're not motivated to ace your exams.

• You hate to get up in the morning to report to class, or hate to go to school after a long day of work.

• You study just enough to get a passing grade and you really don't care.

• You find yourself waiting till the last minute to do assignments, study for exams, and write papers.

• You have a mental tattoo that reads "Complacency is Cool" and it shows daily.

If you are high school student, college student, adult student, online student, or "off for a while" student and the above sounds like you are dealing with APATHY.

1. Apathy is when you **lack EMOTION**.

2. Apathy is when you **lack MOTIVATION**.

3. Apathy is when you **lack ENTHUSIASM.**

4. Apathy is the state of **not CARING**.

5. Apathy is the state of **not WANTING TO KNOW**.

6. Apathy is when you are satisfied with **COMPLACENCY**.

You Are Not Alone

While in graduate school at Lehigh University, pursuing my first Master's degree in Polymer Science and Engineering, "Apathy" was the middle initial in my name "Kantis A. Simmons"

Attending a school in a slow paced city, like Bethlehem, Pennsylvania felt like the wilderness that Jesus was in. Even though Jesus was there for only 40 days, I was there for two years. It was so *wack* there, well at least before I overcame the stress and depression caused by apathy.

I would watch hours of TV, when I should have been in the laboratory working on my thesis. When it was time to read books and scientific journals, I found myself reading sport magazines. This lead to a few weeks of poor results on test, headaches, and weeks of sluggishness. Now this was probably duplicated when I was in high school or even in undergraduate school, but I found a way to constantly pull myself out of the "rut"

You Can Overcome Apathy as a Student

1. Do Something.
When you find yourself not wanting to do anything, do something. Pick up a book, take yourself out on the town, go hang with a good friend, color in a coloring book, or go have a super fun day.

2. Sketch a Picture of Yourself.

Whip out a piece of paper and sketch how you look, and in most cases the image on the piece a paper will be either how you want to look, funny and make u smile, or disgust you on how you presently look. The feelings generated from this picture will help you realize how you actually envision yourself. As a result it will paint for you an internal image of your mindset. "Before you can go forward in life, you must identify where you are."

3. Re-identify or Identify Your Academic Goals.

Take some time to assess why you are school, and what kind of G.P.A. you want to accomplish. Make sure your goals are written, present, personal, and positive. If you need help writing goals or want to know more about setting Academic Goals, then see Play #4 later inthe book.

4. Craft a Clear Vision.

When you don't have a clear vision on something, life can be cloudy. Take some time to write a vision statement of your life purpose. It will help you stay on track.

Here's my vision:

I Kantis Simmons strive to be the leader in information publishing that changes the mindset, attitude, actions and life habits of students and professionals by developing and presenting resources to help them understand their unique and customized purpose and be thoroughly equipped to carry it out in the earth – thus making their lives, their families and their call fruitful.

5. Hang Out With New Friends.

Look in your cell phone, look at your classmates, look at your text buddies, look at your close internet friends. Who's bringing you down? Who's devaluing you? Find some new eagles, and fly with them. Friend Me on Facebook or Twitter, I'm an Eagle. I would love to become your friend, so connect with me or email me at kantis@PlayingYourAgame.com

6. Take Your Failures and Turn Them Into Successes.

Think of a few failures you have had this school term thus far. How can you re-frame those into positive experiences? What did you learn from those experiences that can help you avoid further issues?

7. Find Someone Who's Less Fortunate Than You Are.

There are many people who would love to be where you are right now. Look around and discover just how blessed you are. No matter what your situation, there is something good that you can be thankful for. Don't have a "Pity Party" – have a "Praise Party". Praise all those who have helped you get to where you are today. Send them an email or handwritten postcard to simply say thank you. This would make you feel so good.

8. Get Off Your Rear End.

Like my high school baseball coach would say; "Get the Lead Out Your Butt Kantis" I'm not meaning to be offensive, I'm just telling you what he told me (and it worked). Realize that where you are right now is not your final destination, but it is a point on the path. Keep your left foot continuously moving in front of your right, and run towards your goals. You can do it my friend!

Apathy is nothing to hold on to. If not dealt with, it can lead to stress, depression, defeat, or even suicide.
If you want to reverse apathy, and if you want to keep your motivation high and your grades up, you have to get off the wrong path.

Here are five more tips to help you stay on the path to motivation:

Have A Pep Rally & Keep Your Motivation High

1 - Succeed one semester at a time.

A semester is long enough to give you a chance to develop new skills and habits, but not so long you will lose sight of your goals and slack off. It is a good idea to write down what you want to accomplish by the end of the term. Put down specifically what you want to achieve. Sure, you would like to have straight A's, but is that realistic for you?

Set your grade-goals high enough to give you a challenge, but not impossibly high. If your strengths are in math and science, it may be reasonable to aim for A's there, but smarter to aim for B+ in English which is usually your worst subject.

2 - Organize to achieve your objectives.

You will be tempted to spend most of your time on activities you most enjoy; that's human nature. Resist that temptation by doing your most important and most challenging subjects first. This will keep you moving toward your objectives. Seeing progress will help keep you motivated.

Reward yourself for your work by doing some activity you enjoy. If you hate English, but love science, reward yourself for completing your English homework by some extra time in science. If school generally turns you off, reward yourself for getting your schoolwork done by some time shooting hoops or playing a video game.

3 - Everything has an expiration date.

Keep yourself on track and motivated by setting deadlines for completing work. If you tend to dawdle, try setting a kitchen timer to keep you on task. If you have a big project, break it into smaller steps. Staying motivated is easier when you can see you are moving toward finishing a project.

4 - Keep the prize in front of your eyes.

You cannot keep your eye on the goal unless you can

see it. Use visual reminders of what you intend to accomplish. Put your calendar and to-do list where you can see it easily and often. Use colored markers to indicate what is most important to accomplish.

5 - Hang out with "Cool" people.

If all the kids you hang out with hate school, find teachers boring, and see no point in studying, you are going to have a real struggle to stay motivated. If you are around people who are enthusiastic, work hard, and enjoy what they do, you will find it much easier to be motivated to do your own work.

You do not have to give up all your friends; just do not spend all your free time with kids who discourage you from working toward your objectives.

* NOTE: *You are the average of the 5 people you hang around the most; your G.P.A. is too. So do the math!*

Staying upbeat has less to do with being enthusiastic than it has to do with being persistent. If you keep plodding toward your objectives, you will find staying motivated is not as hard as you thought.

Discover Your "Why?"

People often ask me, why did I go to school all those years and get 3 advanced scientific degrees? What kept you motivated to go to school year after year and continue to report to class semester after semester? I had to understand and discover my WHY?

I had to understand the root to my motive and the root to my motivation. While attending Norfolk State Univeristy, I remember a professor saying "If you want to earn more in life Kantis, then learn more - become a perpetual learner."

That phrase not only took me through grad school but it anchors my mindset right now. I am constantly learning and constantly looking for ways to take action on the things that I have learned.

I understood my "why". My motivation was to earn more. I wanted to earn more wisdom, more opportunities, more experiences, more finances, and more peace. I felt the only way for me to pursue life's assignment was to pursue education as a scientist. Later on I came to realize that it was those years as a scientist that helped me develop my motivation for my journey as an Academic Success strategists, speaker and author.

For you to keep yourself motivated through rigorous semesters and school years, you MUST determine your *why*. You have to define your motive for being in school. You have to clearly state what it is in the future that you want to accomplish. Your known motive will keep you motivated, and that starts with understanding your *why*.

THE GAMEPLAN FOR MOTIVATION
Take the time to think, answer, and take action now!

What do you dislike most about school?

_____

_____

_____

_____

_____

_____

_____

_____

_____

In what ways do you demonstrate that you are dealing with apathy?

_____

_____

_____

_____

_____

_____

As of today, what is your biggest accomplishment in school? Why?

_____

_____

_____

_____

_____

As of today, what is your biggest regret about school?

_____
_____
_____
_____
_____
_____

What Academic Goals do you have for your self? If none, set some here:

_____
_____
_____
_____
_____
_____

What friends can assist you with accomplishing your goals? Name them.

_____
_____
_____
_____
_____
_____

What friends are holding you back from your goal?

_____
_____
_____
_____
_____

Why do you desire to be in school and achieve those goals?

_____
_____
_____
_____
_____
_____
_____
_____
_____
_____

play #2

Set a Winner's Mindset

So What's On Your ipod?

Have you heard the powerful statement, "Attitude Determines your Altitude". Well that statement is so powerful and so true. It is even true where your academic success and school success is concerned.

What's your attitude towards your teachers and professors? Is it negative or is it positive?

What's your attitude towards your grades, your classes, and your classmates?

You are effective based on your positive attitude and defeated based on your negative attitude.

Here are some famous quotes to adjust your attitude on academic success.

> *If you don't like something, change it. If you can't change it, change your attitude. Don't complain.* - Maya Angelou

> *The greatest discovery of my generation is that man can alter his life simply by altering his attitude of mind.* - James Truslow Adams

> *Ability is what you're capable of doing. Motivation determines what you do. Attitude determines how well you do it.* - Lou Holtz

The best way to inspire people to superior performance is to convince them by everything you do and by your everyday attitude that you are wholeheartedly supporting them. - Harold S. Geneen

The greatest discovery of my generation is that human beings can alter their lives by altering their attitudes of mind. - William James

A daily glance in the mirror can tell you what you look like, but a daily adjustment of your attitude can tell you what you will LIVE like. - Kantis A. Simmons

Every Student Can Learn From the "King of Pop" Michael Jackson

Well the media has followed his career from beginning to end, his death was very shocking for the entire world, and now his last appearance can be seen on DVD entitled, Michael Jackson's THIS IS IT. If you have ever seen this movie, I believe you would agree that this movies is very interesting and educational to see.

I can honestly say that I did not plan on even seeing this movie, but I did view it in the movie theaters the very first week it hit the movie theaters...but I'm glad I did.

With my Twizzlers in hand and my large mixed ICEEE at my side (that were both more than my matinee ticket price) I sat in an fairly empty theater zoomed in to see what the rumors were all about.

I can be known to watch things with a critical eye, but today I chose to simply enjoy this movie, which was a 'behind the scenes concert rehearsal capture' directed by Kenny Ortega. "This Is It" was not suppose to be it for Michael Jackson, but instead it produced some great lessons to be learned; especially life lessons and success principles that anyone can use to improve their life.

A FEW RANDOM OBSERVATIONS

Before I share my deep life lessons, maybe you can help me with my random observations. Maybe you had the same thoughts, when viewing the movie. I'm a huge Michael Jackson fan, so let me vent for a quick second.

1. Early in the movie, did it seem like Michael Jackson dancing skills were off? Was MJ getting old? Maybe he was just in 1st gear. Oh my!

2. Did you hear that bass line reprise on the end of "Thriller" That was so hot! OMG!

3. Why was that black coat so big that he was wearing, I'm assuming he borrowed it to stay warm?

4. I loved the little girl holding the world – you must watch the movie all the way through to the end of the credits to see what I'm talking about.

No More Randomness, Lessons For Winners

1 – Have a Strong Personal Coach.

Whatever you plan on doing in life, there is someone who has gone before you and both failed and/or succeeded. All successful people have coaches, mentors or trainers. In this movie, Michael Jackson's Dance Choreographer, Travis Payne, was by his side making sure he had his moves down. We didn't see all of the hands on instruction that goes behind the scenes to his development, but the choreographer was there to make sure he knew where to go next on the stage and what move would be most effective.

In my workshops and speeches, I make reference to other greats like Michael Jordan and Tiger Woods; both had personal coaches to help them get better. If the greatest basketball player and golfer of all time needed a coach, what makes you think you don't need one? Both MJ and MJ did.

If you are pursuing an academic degree, starting a new business, or trying to become a better parent – locate a strong and proven coach that can propel you to the next level. I myself have several coaches that I invest into every year, because I want to get better as a speaker, academic success coach, and author. You should too – I challenge you to locate one.

2 – Your Vision in Life Will Pull Forth Vision Out of Others.

I loved listening to the testimonies of the dancers and

the musicians in the movie. A consistent thought from all of them was that by having the opportunity to work with Michael Jacskon was a big goal or dream of theirs.

One male dancer even mentioned how at a young age he wanted to work with Michael Jackson, and when given the opportunity to audition, he dropped everything he had going to pursue his dance dream.

I'm pretty sure that over Michael Jackson's career, his vision of excellence and his vision to help the entire world caused those around him to enhance and focus their vision. So I ask you, Will your life vision pull vision out of those you work with?

3 – Work Only With The Best.

Every championship team realizes that it takes *total* teamwork to become a champion in their sport; and if you can get the best players to play together on one team then that is almost a sure guarantee for victory.

Like the USA Basketball team has done repeatedly in the World Olympics, Michael Jackson gathered the best of the best to play on his team. From producers, videographers, costume directors, choreographers, staging, lighting and musicians, he hired only the best.

One of my friends and mentors, Jonathan Sprinkles said to me one time,

"Hang with, study with, and coach with the #1 person in any field (not the #2 person), because the #1 person is #1 for a reason."

4 – Have a Bigger Purpose For What You Do in Life.
Even though Michael Jackson was the king of POP, an icon and has had so many songs on the top music charts, his greater purpose was to heal the world – heal how people love one another and how people love the world in which we live in.

What's your greater purpose? Why do you ultimately exist? Why do you do what you do?

As for me, my greater purpose is to enhance the mind-set, attitude, actions and life habits of students and professionals by developing and presenting resources to help them understand their unique and customized purpose. Then be thoroughly equipped to carry it out in the earth – thus making their lives, their families and their calling fruitful.

5 – Capture The Key Moments of Your Life and Learn From Them
At the beginning of the movie, Director Kenny Ortega mentioned that this movie came about because of the video camera that were in rehearsals and the footage was going to go in Michael Jackson's personal private collection.

I'm sure that Michael Jackson was his own biggest critic about his craft and was going to use this footage to analyze himself, analyze his show, and use it to get better at his craft, which is an awesome thing to do.

I myself do this after completing a great talk for a high

school or college. I would sit down and replay the entire footage of my speech. Most time it's painful to watch, because I sincerely want to be the best at what I do when engaging a crowd. I encourage you to capture those key moments in your life. If it's a presentation, performance, event, or simple conversation with someone – use that recorded footage to learn more about yourself and get better.

6 – Stay Teachable and Humble

It is very obvious from his lifetime of music success that Michael Jackson was teachable and understood humility. It was very powerful to see how the music director and production director knew when to submit their idea to Michael Jackson, and Michael's to theirs. I'm pretty sure that his power packed team had a load of great ideas for the concert, but they were willing to adjust and be flexible for the overall objective. It was never about *their* agenda, but about the mission at hand.

7 – Practice, Practice, Practice and then Practice Perfect.

I love seeing MJ do the classic dance routines to his classic songs in the movie, like "Beat It", "Thriller", and "Smooth Criminal". It was very obvious that because of repetition, he was able to do it sweatlessly and flawlessly. It even seemed to me that he had regained his youth when doing those moves, versus other times he looked kind of old and stiff. (Just my randomness again).

Practice does not make perfect, but *perfect and correct practice makes perfect.*

When it comes to school academics, business, or any life endeavor, your preparation phase will always determine your outcome of victory. You may have heard the famous saying, *When preparation meets opportunity it produces success* - which is so true.

Know Your Craft Better Than Anyone Else

The music director and various musicians in the band, said that Michael Jackson knew all of his songs. He knew the key, the tempo, the rhythm of certain riffs. He was a student of his own music and his craft.

Seeing and hearing this on camera instantly made me evaluate my life. As my mind wondered and spanned the years of my existence, I was convicted and yet convinced to simply get better. Know my craft!

You too must daily judge your life and craft. Where do you have cracks? Where are you weak? Where do you need to improve? How are you settling for average when you know that excellence is needed?

If you ever want to do the best, you must consistently do things that will propel you to be the best.

Average people will never fully see the best, because their mindset and actions are like everyone else.

Success is hard, and it is not for the weak. If you want better, then do better. Consistently learn, consistently train, and consistently improve.

So there you have it... The winning lessons I learned from *Michael Jackson's This Is It*.

Now I'm sure that if you have seen the movie, there's a lot that you learned from it as well. Feel free to send me an email to comment on Michael Jackson's movie. I would love to see if you are a big fan like me.

Productivity - The Key to Academic Winners

So lets talk about productivity. What it is, why it's important, and how you can achieve it.

Productivity is about results, it about creating tangible, real world, real life actual results. It's not about doing a lot of work, or pretending you are getting it done, but its about getting results in the real world - and your real world is SCHOOL.

I'm going to teach you a technique here about maximizing your productivity in school and in your everyday life. It's a simple technique, regardless of whether you are in elementary school or grad school, this technique will work for anyone.

Now the first distinction that I want to draw is that between activity and results. You will hear me talk about this throughout this book, but it's very easy to confuse activity and results. Some may think that doing a bunch of activity means things are getting done. This can be a problem if you don't understand the difference.

While in corporate America, as a research scientist I had to learn that there is a major difference. I was at one time just doing my job, and not realizing that at my level in my career, the company was paying me to kick out RESULTS. I'm glad to say that I eventually got it right, and produced two major contact lens products for the company.

In some cases, people see RESULTS as the enemy to their career.

I heard this story about a mailman who replaced a previous mailman who had worked on a particular route for 30 years. The new mailman would do the same route, and deliver all his mail and be done by the middle of the day. Then he would return back to his post office around lunch, and say *"I'm done with my route."* All the other mailman would look at him and say, *"Noooo Way! Figure how to take longer in doing your route, because you are making all of us look bad, by getting it done so fast. If you don't, we are going to give you so much trouble"*, and the postal worker said to himself, *"Oh I see, these men are just seeing this as a job where they are paid for time, and not for results."*

Now these men, didn't want to have their day threatened because they were using their day for personal things and casually having fun all during the time while they were on their job. So results are an enemy to their "job" mentality.

The same can be true, where you are just going to school just to get to the next grade, and not going their to get results. Or better yet, to get true understanding of the subject matter, so you can be skilled in a certain field when you graduate.

So how do you get around this?

The technique I want to share with you right now to maximize results is deceptively simple. So simple that you will say, "Wow, I wish I would have know this all my life." I believe, that as you start using this, you will see just how amazing it is.

The idea is to measure productivity visually.

Let's say that you want to lose weight, and you don't know specifically how much you weigh, but you get on the scale everyday and find that sometimes you weigh a couple of pounds more and sometimes you weigh a couple of pounds less, depending on what you ate or what you drunk. Depending on what time during the day, and what you were wearing while on the scale.

So we really can't see how much we are losing day to day because of all of the factors.

On the other hand, if you take a simple spreadsheet like Microsoft Excel, Google Documents or even take a piece of paper and create a table, and then everyday weigh your self and place the weight on the spread-sheet.

Do this every day. Weigh yourself, and write your weight down on the table or spread sheet, and then graph the numbers where you can make a visual graph of your results day to day. Pictorially you can see the ups and downs over a period of a week and you can see the variations. But by looking at this graph, you can see the direction that it is going. You can visually see if it is going up, flat or if it is going down. You can see it clearly. Hopefully, since your goal is to lose weight, then the lines should be decreasing and going down. The visual feedback does its own work. It builds its own aware-ness, it creates direction all by itself.

I used this technique with not only things I did in the science lab, but I also used this technique while chart-ing my school grades and G.P.A.. I would record my grades for every class, and put it on x-y graph and then visually chart the progress. This easily helped me see if my grades and test scores were going up, or were they going down.

Today, I even use this where my business is concerned to chart the impact and the number of people I am reaching with my message. In whatever you do, you can use this to chart finances, hours of study, physical fitness goals, or progress in a certain school class. By having this visual chart, you can easily see what is go-ing on.

If you look at a column of numbers, there's no way to chart it in your mind or try to kind of figure it out, but when you see a chart or graph of the actual progress (with the up and down lines), the whole thing speaks very loudly.

I think that this idea of the Visual Display of quantitative information, or the charting of numbers is one of the biggest innovations that we have ever had.

Chart It

So if you want to dramatically improve your productivity as a student, then take the time to chart the top three areas in your life or the top three classes where you desire improvement and productivity, and figure out how to put it on a chart.

So lets say you want to improve your study skills, put down how many hours of consistent studying you did every single day. Then chart it out over a month. Let's say you want to finish an end of the year project, go ahead and chart how many hours per day you worked uninterrupted and un-distracted to research or write the paper for that project.

If you want to track your test scores, put the results of your graded test or quizzes on a chart, so you can visually see if you are bound for an A+ grade. Things that are measured, are improved.

Here is a great quote...

Processes that are measured improve; and processes that are measured and reported improve exponentially.

So if you really want to get some juice out of this technique, keep record and chart your results, and then report it to someone else, you will see it drastically improve.

That is why report cards are so important in the school year, but if you visually put your grades on a pictorial graph, everything inside of you will start to work to get things to improve.

Have you ever heard that a picture is worth a thousand words?

Well that picture will help push you to be more productive in the classroom, out of the classroom, and in every aspect of your life. Now that's one great technique to dramatically improve your productivity, by visually charting your results.

Winners do simple things like this!

THE GAMEPLAN FOR A
WINNER'S MINDSET

Take the time to think, answer, and take action now

What negative thoughts or words continually haunt you? The ones from you and the ones from others?

_____
_____
_____
_____
_____
_____

Which of the above do you honestly believe and why?

_____
_____
_____
_____

What positive thoughts or words continually encourage you? The ones from you and the ones from others?

_____
_____
_____
_____
_____
_____
_____

Who are your mentors and personal coaches? And why did you select each of them?

_____
_____
_____
_____
_____
_____
_____

Who do you want to be your personal mentor? What attribute(s) do they have, that you want for your yourself?

_____
_____
_____
_____
_____
_____
_____
_____
_____
_____
_____
_____

What areas do you find yourself very productive?

_____
_____
_____
_____

_____
_____
_____
_____
_____
_____

What areas do you see your self unproductive?

_____
_____
_____
_____
_____
_____

Detail 10 things you can do over the next 30 days that will make you a more productive person.

_____
_____
_____
_____
_____
_____
_____
_____
_____
_____
_____
_____
_____
_____

Write down 5 positive statements about your self that can enhance your confidence to reach all of your set goals

_____

_____

_____

_____

_____

_____

_____

_____

_____

_____

play #3

See School As Your
Full-Time Job

———————————————————

Let Us Talk About Time Management

First of all, I want to share a quote from Stephen Covey, the author of *7 Habits of Highly Effective People*. Stephen is a genius and he says,

"Time management is a misnomer - the challenge is to manage ourselves".

You can't actually manage time, it runs at the same speed, no matter what you decide to do. So you can't actually manage time; but what you can do is learn to manage yourself.

The big challenge in this day and age is to manage ourselves. We are dealing with all kinds of challenges that we haven't had to deal with before.

Al Reis and Jack Trous, authors of the book Positioning said, "we live in today's first over communicated society", meaning there is too much communication and information coming in. Now they wrote that book and said that back in 1980 - even before the internet was created, before we had cell phones, and before we had stuff like text messages, Facebook, Twitter, YouTube, and video chat. It was written before all of these direct access communications where you can get in touch with someone 24 hours a day - 7 days a week.

Now if we were the world's first over communicated society then, back in 1980, where do you think we are

69

now? SUPER OVERLY communicated with.

Where we are now is we are completely drowning in communication, we are drowning in information, we are drowning in distraction, interruption and are over-loaded by all the things that are happening.

And in order to confront this, as a student you can't look at everything, you can't watch everything, you can't do everything, and you can't take advantage of every op-portunity at school. You have to become very selective.

When we talk about time management and productivity in school, we are talking about *self management,* and getting ourselves to do the things, which are the most important things.

You will discover, that if you just focus on a *few* key important things and do them over and over and over, the rest will take care of itself. If you eat simple meals of healthy food, and do a little bit of simple exercises every day, health just takes care of itself.

If you invest quality time in an open dialogue one on one with your parents, teachers, or friends on a regular basis, the relationship will take care of itself.

That's the way things work. But we don't do these things... what we do instead is eat a bunch of snacks, eat a bunch of junk food, and forget to exercise.

Or we pick up our phones and make a quick call to say, "Hey how you doing?", or "I love you", and you think that is quality time?

Or even worse, you sit down with someone and while talking to them, you are text messaging, on the computer, watching television, and missing out on that clear intimate valuable conversation that is connecting.

Now the above is what destroys health and relationships. The same thing destroys productivity and it destroys getting the results you desire in school and in life.

When we focus on just those few things that are important, and figure out how to get ourselves to behave to focus on those things, that's when life really begins to turn around.

Interestingly enough, I have discovered that time management comes down to setting conditions in your life that make it so you can't do anything but focus on the important things. It's not about making a list of things to do, or a check list and doing the right thing, yet that can be important sometimes. It's about setting up your life and environment so that you automatically do the things that are important and you do not have the option to do other things.

For example, when you first sit down to study and do class work, don't check your voicemail and email

- work on your most important school subjects. Work on something that will produce the highest return in your week. Something that's going to make your week more successful.

Here's what most students do...they check their email, they check their voicemail, and they get on Facebook and see what everyone else is doing socially. Now that completely takes over their time.

Here's something else that can be done. Set aside entire hours of time, where you only focus on one school subject at a time. Focus on those subjects that are the most challenging and the ones that need the most attention.

Another thing we need to train ourselves to do is invest time in focused uninterrupted blocks. Now this is an idea that all of the great time management gurus teach. They suggest focusing on one thing for an extended period of time. Cultivate the ability to focus your mind. When you are focused on one thing for an extended period of time and you block out all the distractions and interruptions, you don't have anything to do, but that one thing.

This thought mimics something like, sitting in a clean room, with no windows, no distractions, and your class book and notes - focused solely on that class assignment for large amounts of time.

So time management, what is it?

It's all about managing yourself, not about managing your time. It's about learning how to develop healthy habits and rituals so that you do the right things every day and it's about setting up the conditions in your life, physically, emotionally, and logically, so that you're forced to do the right things and you don't have any other options.

So get to work right now doing the right things every day, and creating an environment that blocks out interruptions and distractions, so you just stay focused. If you just do that one thing, create an environment that blocks out distractions and interruptions and keep you focused on those few important school things, you will see your productivity in school sky rocket immediately.

School Is Your Occupation

Do you realize that from the age of 5 years old, all youth are enrolled in school? And most likely, you have been in school or working on some of kind of degree since that time period.

I want to impress upon you that being in school/education is your FULL TIME OCCUPATION. You should see it that way until you achieve your degree or educational goals.

73

Just like a typical employee checks in to their job at 8 AM and checks out at 5 PM, I have composed a lists of things you should consider when planning and scheduling your work day as a student.

Schedule quiet, motivational time. Visualize the success of your day before the actual day occurs by reading, meditating, praying, and or having your personal "pep-rally".

1. Allocate the times you must be in class on a specific day.

2. Define the time periods in which you will study.

3. Plan for breakfast and lunch, but don't eat for longer than 30 minutes, use the other designated half hour to prepare for your next class.

4. Set time aside for part time jobs, extracurricular activities, and other necessary events.

5. Carry a detailed appointment book or organizer, so you will always know what needs to be done for the day.

6. Communicate your study times to friends and family, so they are aware of your schedule and won't interfere.

7. Go to your study periods as if you have an

important appointment.

8. Designate a specific location outside your bedroom to study each subject. Study location can differ based on mood, surrounding, and time of day.

9. Plan your free time as you wish.

10. Establish your play time. Don't be a workaholic.

11. Study for the designated class at the designated time, even if you don't have a test or homework assignment.

12. Don't allow planned activities to overlap, schedule it on purpose then do it on purpose. (When it's time to read, read. When it's time to work, work; and when it's time to study, study).

Have a Successful Hour

For you to have a success in your occupation, let's break things down to first having a having a successful hour.

If you can have 24 consecutive successful hours you can have a successful day.

Seven successful days will produce a successful week.

If you can put 52 good weeks together, you will have a successful year. But the root to your successful year begins with what? "A successful HOUR".

Here are 5 things you can do to have a productive hour.

1. Recognize the importance and value of 60 minutes.

Time cannot be regained once it's lost or misused. However the well use of time can produce a day of joy and sense of accomplishment.

2. Detail and plan EVERY minute of your hour.

Have you ever thought about how many pages you can read in a book in 60 minutes? Have you considered how much studying can be accomplished in one hour? Allocate a to-do item for every minute in your hour. Then stick to it.

3. Identify Time Wasters and alleviate them.

What acts in your day are stealing your time and making your day unfruitful? Is it Tv? Daydreaming? Certain people? The internet? Whatever it may be, make the adjustment and either cancel it, or schedule it on purpose in your hourly schedule.

4. Stay focused on hourly agendas that you have set.

If you plan to study, study! If you plan to be in class, be fully attentive in class. If you plan to socialize, socialize. Whatever you plan to do in the hour, apply discipline and focus to stick with it.

5. Win at the present hour.

Perform the previous 4 steps for the present hour. Then do the same for the next 23 hours.

Once It's Gone, You Can't Get It Back

Managing time, budgeting time, and utilizing the 24 hours accurately is a mandatory skill to develop if you want to succeed academically and beyond. In the 4th part of our Academic Survival Skill Series we will look at time management - how successful studying starts with budgeting your time.

Recently, I was speaking to a friend of mine who is raising a family, working a forty hour a week job, and receiving her Master's degree. And she simply said, *"Kantis, I need more time!"*

Now you and I know we can't get more time, but only use the time we have effectively.

In your quest to improve your grades, live your life and get it all done within 24 hours a day, here are a few "time tips" below:

- Develop a schedule that includes all "regular" activities, such as classes, a part time job, meals, family, or practices (with an athletic team or group).

- Reserve time for sleep, exercising, and recreation.

- Schedule review time for right after a lecture or right before a discussion if possible.

- Plan ahead for all major projects and exams. Don't wait until the last minute.

- Break up all your tasks and set them as time goals (Goal #1- search sources, Goal #2- review notes, etc.).

- Attempt to study the same subject at the same time each day.

- Take short breaks to reward yourself - you deserve it.

THE WINNER'S SCHEDULE

Take the time to think, answer, and take action now.

Use the area below to draft your weekly schedule.

List all the things you have to do in a day, all the things you must do in a week, and all the things you must do in a month. Implement your study time, class, time, family time, and social time.

_____

_____

_____

_____

_____

_____

_____

_____

_____

_____

_____

_____

_____

_____

_____

_____

_____

_____

_____

_____

_____

_____

_____

79

Playing Your A Game

(continue your schedule....)

_____

_____

_____

_____

_____

_____

_____

_____

_____

_____

_____

_____

_____

_____

_____

_____

_____

_____

_____

_____

_____

_____

_____

_____

_____

_____

_____

play #4

See Your Bulls-Eye and Hit It

Stretch for the Mark

Let's assume a Chemistry course is based on the following grading assignment percentage:

Tests 50%
Quizzes 30%
Homework 10%
Class Participation 8%
Final Project 2%

What portion of the Chemistry grade do you think the average student will neglect if he is pressed for time and energy? He will most likely neglect the final project, because it is only worth a small amount of the overall grade.

I have learned that this two percent makes the difference between making an "A" or a "B." Whatever class you are in press toward the goal, and always shoot for the best. Press forward and eagerly pursue the prize - the best you can get in school is an "A," so press for an "A."

Here are some helpful pointers as you strive towards the best.

• Be prepared for and arrive to class on time.

• Sit near the front of the classroom to avoid distractions, and get better grades. Reports show that stu-

students who sit in the "T" (the first few rows, and the section in the middle of the classroom), get better grades automatically, and is more noticed by the teacher.

• Ask questions when needed for clarity sake.

• Participate in class discussions.

• Try to stay ahead (or current) in your reading and class notes.

• Be and stay alert. Stay focused on the professor's lecture and content - especially when he or she is very passionate about a certain topic. This here
is clear giveaway of what's going to be on your next text.

• Attempt to complete all homework problems or helpful exercises. Even if they're difficult, give it your best shot (they just might show up on a future test).

• Take advantage of the professor's office hours. Introduce yourself and continue to show your teacher that you desire to learn this information by reporting to their office hours (Your consistency will help you get a higher grade especially if your grades are on the borderline).

• Attempt to understand all the content given or required for the class.

• Don't ever give up. Quitters never see their "A" Game.

Shoot for the best even when it is a small percentage of the overall grade. That small percentage may be what's needed for your "A".

Apply the Law of DCD

Be (D)isciplined, (C)onsistent, and (D)iligent at all costs.

Discipline - 1. (n) training expected to produce a specific character or pattern of behavior, especially training that produces moral or mental improvement. 2. (v) To impose order upon.

Consistency - Conforming to the same principles or course of action repeatedly over a period of time.

Diligence - 1. Persistent application to one's occupation or studies. 2. To be eager, to operate in forwardness and earnestness.

After 25 years of formal education, this is the one 'play' that either granted me success or failure. It is the Law of D-C-D that will put you on top. Without this principle, you will have a hard time playing your "A" Game.

After enjoying a beautiful and busy weekend with my wife, family or friends, a Monday morning class was the last thing on my mind in grad school. My body and soul would sometimes say, "Forget about that 8:00am class."

Can you relate to this?

You will have to overcome those emotional road blocks and set up some boundaries for D-C-D to work.

D-C-D says...

I am going to go to class, I am going to go study.

I am going to keep reading no matter what it takes.

I am going t keep working on writing my essays.

I am going to study and complete those homework problems.

I am going to keep doing what brought me success.

I will discipline myself even when everyone else wants to go to parties or hangout at the movies.

This play of D-C-D encourages you to stay focused on your goals and desires until they are accomplished.

In my second year of college, I made a decision to operate by D-C-D and achieve a 4.0 for that semester. At that time, I would go to class and then hop in bed and sleep the rest of the afternoon. At about 11:00PM, I would get up and study until the morning, shower for class, and repeat the cycle again.

Life was so peaceful that semester. The dorms were always quiet, because when I was sleeping, everyone was in class or at the library, and when I was studying, they were sleeping. You may think this schedule was weird, but I enjoyed it for what it was worth.

Keep in mind that discipline, consistency, and diligence can interfere with your social life if you do not first communicate your academic goals with your friends.

Once, I changed a movie date with a young lady because of my focused goals. Rather than going to a night movie, I asked her if we could go to a matinee. In fact, there were many times when we had to go out for breakfast instead of dinner because 1) I was disciplined with my time and 2) I went to bed early with the intention of studying when everyone else was asleep.

As you can probably imagine, this crazy schedule did not give me much success with her but it did help me get a 4.0 that semester. I am not advising that you sleep during the day and work at night; however, I am suggesting that you remain consistent and diligent in doing the things that you had planned to do that week.

The best time for you to study is when you feel your super powers.

What time of day are you most energetic? What time of day do you feel a sense of urgency and clarity? Whenever that time is for you, that is the time to focus in and start studying those harder and more demanding class subjects.

I have also noticed in my personal life that order or the lack thereof effects D-C-D.

It is interesting, but I have realized that when my bedroom or home is disorderly, then my life is disorderly.

The same was true for my school notebooks. When my class notebooks were well organized, I found that D-C-D was in place. But when they were chaotic, things in my academic life were out of wack as well too.
Is this a good representation of what's in your life? Is your room dirty and in disarray? Are your notebooks organized? What does this say about
your personal life?

Are you operating by D-C-D? I encourage you to make a personal decision to remain disciplined, consistent, and diligent. Take some time to evaluate your present weaknesses and shortcomings, then develop a plan of improvement.

So What's Your Goal?
When you think about achieving SUCCESS, you have to think about setting and achieving GOALS.

When you think about achieving ACADEMIC SUC-CESS, you must think about setting and achieving AC-ADEMIC GOALS.

Achieving SUCCESS EQUALS setting and achieving GOALS.

You cannot achieve success without working towards something that is measurable, memorable and attainable. Goals allow you to gauge when you have achieved success.

During my sophomore year of college, I received a 4.0 GPA.

How did I achieve academic success that year? I learned the power of setting academic goals.

Because I set this goal, I had to develop various academic survival skills like taking notes, studying for exams, and knowing how to listen in class. I had to change specific academic and social habits in order to achieve success. I changed my study habits, my sleeping patterns and even my dating routine - yes "girls" had to take the back seat.

I achieved academic success that year because I set an academic goal and this goal became the motor (or motive) behind how I functioned as a student and today you can do the same. What I mean is this…

By establishing academic goals that are PRESENT, POSITIVE, and PERSONAL, all the required academic survival skills of listening in class, taking great notes, class participation, etc. will become the needed actions to support the goal you have initially set for yourself. They become the action steps required to achieve your goals.

How to Set Goals and Accomplish Them

Lets talk about how to set goals and how to accomplish them.

Goal Setting is one of the most talked about areas of personal development and self development areas, and it is one of the things that people do the least. Everyone has heard that you got to set goals, you need to set goals, you gotta set goals, set goals; yet most people don't do them. Why?

Well, I think there are a couple of reasons why people don't set goals, and I think there are a few simple techniques to set goals and accomplish them.

Why don't we set goals?

If we know they are so important, then why do we avoid it?

There was a book written several years ago called,

Stop Setting Goals If You Would Rather Solve Problems, and its a book by Bob Biehl.

In the book he talks about this idea, that most people are not motivated by setting goals. Something like 80 % of people, when you say set goals, their eyes glaze over and say, "Ugh that doesn't sound fun at all.

But if you say to them, "I have a problem, can you help me solve it? Or "Here's a list of problems we need to solve" or "Can you find someone to help me solve the problem?" The people will now leap into action, they love solving problems.
You see they don't like to set goals, they only like to solve problems. And maybe that's why only 20% of people are motivated by goal setting.

So, since we just recognized that a lot of us, would rather solve problems than set goals, that frees up a lot of energy to realize it is not just about goal setting, and there are more ways to look at this.

Another reason why people don't set goals is that they just don't know how or ever learned the technique for setting goals. And I would like to introduce a technique to you for setting goals that I feel will be very valuable to you.

When instructed to set goals or make a list of all your goals, what most people do is that they take out there pen and paper, and they sit there and look at their pa-

paper and say:

> *I want to be happy*

> *I want a 4.0.*

> *I want some money for college.*

> *I want my parents and teachers to stop nagging me.*

Most people, let alone students, do not understand the reality of what would happen if they created a vision for their life, if they created an outcome, or if they could see it clearly and make it happen. They are not in touch with all of the other implications that would have on their life.

A much better way is to use this powerful tool called your brain and your mind, and use them to help you set goals.

Before you ever pick up your pen and paper, and write your goals down, it's so important to use this vast tool that you have to imagine what your life would be like if you had or accomplished certain things or had relationships with certain people.

If when I said, "give me a list of all of your goals", and instead of taking a pen and paper and writing down a big list of your goals one by one, you just stop and close your eyes and you start to imagine different scenarios in your mind:

What if I accomplish this outcome?

What if I had a relationship with this person?

What if I was able to achieve this or what if I got this thing in my life?

and then ask...

What are all the other things that would happen afterwards?

What would this thing lead to?

What would that trigger?

Imagine that this is a domino in my life, and what other dominos would I knock down automatically?

And what you would realize is that, by thinking about it for a while and using your imagination power to think big, you'll come up with some great goals to achieve.

Most people would just go grab some paper and start to write down.

I want this, and I want that. Or say, I want a new car,

But STOP! You have to ask yourself, *"What if I get a new car, what will happen in my life?*

And when you ask that question, you may say, "Well I have a new car, its enjoyable to drive, it's nice showing it to other people" and then you will realize after a month or two later, that you are going to get used to your new car and you're going to be making a bigger car payment, and you know that you are going to lose the thrill in having it, and it really isn't going to mean that much to you.

Plus the car you have is fine, now you might realize that.

On the other hand, the goal might be to develop a relationship with a particular mentor in your life, and you might start thinking about that and the purpose of building a relationship with that mentor was to develop to the next level, you'll learn a whole bunch of things that you wouldn't have known before and they'll introduce you to more influential and powerful people. You'll be able to get mentored by some of their friends that will increase your income and you personal satisfaction. Now that's a real big goal, and that's something you really need to figure how to get to do.

Simple Steps to Goal Setting

Use the power of the mind to imagine all the outcomes that will happen.

Next if you relate to the problem solvers, take the goal

that you set, and make a list of all the problems that you need to solve to reach the goal. For problem solvers, it's good to go out into the far future as if the goal is already accomplished, and then work backwards and think about all the problems that need to be solved to get to the ultimate goal. This can be a very useful way for problem solvers to make a list of things they need to do in order to reach their goal.

So goal setting and problem solving is like two different muscles, and we want to work on the both of them.

We don't just want to jump to making a list of things that we want, we want to really use our minds to figure out, if we reach this goal then what will it mean to me. Once we have found a goal that will explode our lives in the most positive way, and will bring us more and more of what we want, then we need to think about that and consider that seriously as a goal to set for ourselves. Then once we have set that goal, we want to back track and go out in the future and then look back to see all the problems that I had to solve on the way to creating this goal.

I want to say one more thing here...

If you really want to make it, so that you reach your goals, ask yourself the questions, *"What conditions must I set up in my life so that the outcome or the goal I want to achieve will happen automatically? How must I set that condition up, so that it's just going to happen automatically?"*

Now that's one of my favorite questions because it takes you up a level. You actually go "meta" and zoom out and you are looking at the situation as a whole, and rather than just saying, "Alright, how do I get this 4.0 thing?" You're saying "What conditions I have to set up to accomplish a 4.0 in my life?"

The conditions can be relationships with people, they can be set ups where you do this one thing, and it causes this other thing to happen.

Conditions can be a lot of different things in this physical environment, relationships, emotionally, and when you ask what conditions must I set to make this goal happen automatically, it just causes you to think on a different level. When you do that, it will make accomplishing the goal a lot easier.

Use those two techniques to set goals and watch yourself accomplish them a lot faster.

Do You Have Goals?

What is it that you want to accomplish in school?

What is it that you want to accomplish in life?

What do you consider to be successful?

96

How do you measure the success of a good school year?

Now what are you willing to adjust for your goals?
My favorite book, the Bible says, "Where there is no vision the people perish" and it also says "write the vision and make it plain, so that all who see it can run with it". Your goals are your vision. And your vision helps you focus on the final destination.

Your goals are like the final destination on Map Quest.

To clarify setting academic goals and accomplishing them...

Here are 7.25 Things to Consider in Your Goal Setting program

1. Your academic goals must be personal.

What do YOU really want to accomplish? What is it that YOU desire in school? What do YOU desire from your social activities? What do YOU desire for your life? Not what someone else wants you to desire.

2. Your academic goals must not contradict any of your other goals.

Your goals must coincide in what is realistically possible. It is unrealistic to set this goal, "I have an overall 4.0 G.P.A., when I graduate from school" if you have already completed a few semesters with a 2.5 GPA. Mathematically, there is no way to accomplish this goal. Setting unrealistic goals is setting realistic failure.

3. Your academic goals must be specific.

Develop goals that are measurable; ones that can be reported and charted over time. Here's an example: "I read two books a month that are nonschool related."

4. Your academic goals must be positive.

Positive goals help your subconscious carry out the goals stated. Your mind and subconscious should only interpret positives. Words like "not", "never", or "no" should be erased so your subconscious can produce the wisdom to carry out only positive goals. Rather than saying, "I will NOT fail this test" say "I make a minimum of 90% on this exam."

5. Your academic goals must be set high, but reachable.

There's a famous quote that says, "If you shoot for the moon and miss, you will still land amongst the stars." Set your goals really high, so that it forces you and stretches you to do better.

6. Your academic goals must be present-tense.

Set goals in the present tense. Past-tense and future-tense goals cause your mind to think in the past and the future. This keeps your goals locked in the past and in the future. Set goals that are present where your subconscious can work as if the goal is already achieved. "As a man thinks so is he". Think positive, personal, and present.

7. Your academic goals must be clearly written.

Using the notes above, make sure you specify your goals on paper. Write them down legibly. Studies have shown that people who write goals are 50-80% closer to attaining them than those who haven't written them down.

7.25. Your academic goals must be connected with practical actions.

For every goal you set, identify some practical things that you can do every day to help you obtain that goal. If you set a goal like the one above,to make 90% on the test, then you must have an action plan. To obtain this goal, actions like spending two hours a day studying, visiting your teacher once a week, reading other books on the subject matter and working extra subject problems. These are the actions to your goals.

GOALS TO YOUR "A" GAME

Take the time to think, answer, and take action now based on the
information you have read above.

How would you feel if you accomplished your biggest
goal?

_____
_____
_____
_____
_____
_____
_____
_____
_____
_____

What will this goal produce for you if you accomplish
it?

_____
_____
_____
_____
_____
_____
_____
_____
_____
_____

Write out your 10 biggest goals, and make them positive, personal, and in the present tense.

1.

2.

3.

4.

5.

6.

7.

8.

9.

10.

play #5

Sharpen Your Focus

"Focus People Focus!"

That's the phrase I hear running through my mind every time I set my desire to do something, and find myself getting distracted.

This too is the phrase I remember hearing the Drama Director shout when I kept messing up my theatrical lines in the production "Spunk" while in graduate school at Lehigh University.

"Focus People Focus!"

This is the phrase that I want to tattoo on your mind, for it is the root cause for low academic performance and sub par school grades. It's also the foundational reason successful people are successful – they know HOW to focus.

With so many things going on in our society, with access to so many resources, with varying life responsibilities, and not to name all this Twitter, Facebook, and YouTube stuff on the internet (in which I'm all on), FOCUS can be challenging for the everyday student.

Whether you are a high school student, a college student, online student, or an adult student raising a family while working a full-time job I have something for you.

Before I give you these essential ways to focus better

while studying, here are a few motivators to support my claims:

> *"When you write down your ideas you automatically focus your full attention on them. Few if any of us can write one thought and think another at the same time. Thus a pencil and paper make excellent concentration tools."* – **Michael Leboeuf**

> *"One reason so few of us achieve what we truly want is that we never direct our focus; we never concentrate our power. Most people dabble their way through life, never deciding to master anything in particular."* - **Anthony Robbins**

> *"If you stay focused and right on track, you will get to where you want to be."* - **Michelle C. Ustaszeski**

> *"The sun's energy warms the world. But when you focus it through a magnifying glass it can start a fire. Focus is so powerful!"* – **Alan Pariser**

Maintain Focus On What You're Working On

So let's talk about how to keep ourselves focused and maintain that focus.

As I learned from Tony Schwartz, the co-author of The Power of Full Engagement (which I recommend you read), the greatest power of the human mind is to focus on one thing at a time. Now we all know that we can only keep one thought or one idea in our conscious mind and well focusing on one thing over an extended period of time is what gives us great leverage. It allows us to get a lot done in our lives.

The problem in the modern day is that there are a lot of distractions and interruptions and other things competing for our attention, so we lose focus, and the great tragedy is not that we are losing focus, it's that we are losing the ability to focus.

So the first thing you must do if you want to maintain focus is to practice maintaining focus.

One of the most valuable lessons, I've learned about time management is to *focus on one thing at a time for an extended period of time.* I originally learned this from Peter Druckert, then later learned more about this from my mentors Gideon Shalwick and Josh Shipp.

The idea is that if and when you focus on one thing you get a lot more done, and becomes a compounding effect. So the best thing to do is to set aside blocks of time, I recommend 60 to 90 minutes minimum.

I like to work in blocks of time of an hour, an hour, then a 15 minute break, because the hour, and a couple fifteen minute breaks, then an hour, and a couple fifteen minute break, it really operates with your natural rhythm of your body.

Plus this rhythm also works with the traditional class school schedule. You are normally in class for an hour, take a small break, then in class for another hour.

One little secret that can dramatically increase your ability to focus is to schedule the breaks that you take. Earnest Rossie, wrote a great book called the Twenty Minute Break and the idea is that our bodies go through these rhythms where we have high energy and low energy, and in the book he talk about every 90 minutes you want to take a break. That's why I like to work for an hour, another hour, then a 30 minute break. Because it optimizes every two and half hours, where you can eat a meal, relax, go for a walk, to take a longer break. But some where in that 90 - 120 minutes, schedule a break for yourself, so that your body can relax and your mind can tune out and so your emotions can recover. When you schedule your breaks, you will come back much more focused and stronger.

So to maintain focus, you need to get rid of the distraction and interruption, then schedule time blocks to work for an hour, to ninety minutes or 120 minutes ideally. And then very importantly, schedule and take regular breaks.

You are honoring the way your system works and you will come back very strong from those breaks and maintain your focus for longer periods of time. Let me say this, as an Academic Success Strategist who speaks to students at educational events, youth conferences and college events, and run an online internet business, lead a family, and author books – FOCUS is still a challenge for me, but as I reflect back, FOCUS has produced some great things in my life pertaining to my own academic success and still does today. It can do the same and more for you.

If you have issues staying focused while studying, do this:

1. State Your Desired Goal
When you go into any study session, if it's at home alone, on campus at the library, or in a group session – state your goals. At the beginning of your study time, write down what you desire to accomplish during this study time. (It may seem nerd-ish, but the group will love you for it too)

2. Set a Time Frame for Intentional Focus
When you make a decision to study your school work, set a specific allotted time to focus. On purpose write down, *For the next _____ Minutes I focus on_____ only.* By writing this down, this helps you to stick to the desired goal at hand and it triggers your mind to be intentional.

3. Declare Your Reward for Intentional Focus
Rewarding yourself is a great motivator for focusing for a set period of time. For example, you can reward yourself by simply taking 10 minutes to enjoy something you love... playing a video game, talking to your

bf, chatting on the internet, eating ice cream, or whatever you desire. The key is to make sure your compensation is relative to what you achieved. After you reward yourself, then get back to focusing.

4. Turn Off All Distractions

This seems obvious right? But I have found that distractions are the #1 enemy to you accomplishing any goal, and our goal is to focus on the school assignment. Therefore turn it all off...the TV, the iPod, the stereo, the cell phone, the internet, the tweets, the pokes, the video games, everything. Even go so far to let your family, friends, and classmates know.

"For the next _____ minutes, I need to completely focus on studying so leave me a message or I will get with you at later specific time." (That's a great voice mail greeting or Facebook status)

5. Remove Clutter and Keep Things Clean

Dr. Laurence J. Peter once said, *"If a cluttered desk is the sign of a cluttered mind, what is the significance of a clean desk?"*

By simply cleaning your work area or study area it allows your mind to be clear, which will also eliminate distractions.

6. Gather Only the Resources You Need For Studying. This is self explanatory but I must stress to only have in front of you everything that you need for one

specific subject. If it doesn't relate with the class you are studying for, remove it completely from your study area.

7. Read Through All Your Written Notes From Beginning to End

To maximize most of your study sessions, start from the beginning reading all of your study notes aloud, and highlight the areas that you will need to spend more intentional focus time on. Make sure you don't stop but continue to move forward with your notes, then review those trouble areas.

7.25. Read Textbooks and Other Resources, Work Problems, and Review All Notes To Enhance Comprehension

Here's where you spend the majority of your study time. After doing the above 7 steps with discipline, you will find that as you go through this step your retention of information will be better, because you are now completely zoned in.

As I echo my Drama Director, "Focus People Focus!"

You Can Write Your School Papers Faster

Just the other day I heard my family members having a "family vent" session. Two women discussing all they have going on in life, and one discussing the many pa-

papers she has to write for class – three to be exact.

After hearing her frustration, I instantly started pondering... "Why did she wait until the last minute? Why is she up late and now thinking about writing her three papers for class that are due the next few days?"

Now before I pass judgment on my kin, I too remember the nights of cramming, stressing, and beating myself up for waiting until the last minute...it really is painful, and it ALWAYS causes you to come up short.

Now back to my kin folk... as aggressive of a woman she is, as passionate of a mother she is, as wonderful of a wife she is...she's enrolled as an online student finishing a Master's degree.

Like myself, you can possibly relate to this mother who is in school, trying to hold down her family, and complete various writing assignments for class.

Well here's a great strategy to write your papers faster and get it done quicker. I used this technique when completing my Master's thesis, authoring all my books, and used it to write various articles and blogs on my websites.

I'm writing this present chapter in this book right now on my blackberry in a crowded room of people watching Saturday night College football while I apply this very technique.

Now this simple technique, has already proven to benefit my family member – she used it to complete those papers that night, and is trying to discipline herself to use it for the weekly papers she will have in the future. So what's the writing technique right?

Before I reveal the technique, note there is cool computer software that you can purchase online to assist you with this concept as well. I will give a few recommendations below.

Here's some simple steps to complete your writing assignments faster:

1. Open up a blank computer document or pull out a blank sheet of paper.

2. Brainstorm and think about what you are about to write, imagine your thoughts from beginning to end.

3. Start typing and writing without stopping. Type consistently without going backwards or pausing to make any edits or correct spelling errors.

4. Fully empty your mind and conscience with all the thoughts concerning your writing assignment... just don't stop writing, until you get to the end or a great stopping point.

5. Re-read the paper and while you read, edit all quickly noticeable errors and misspelled words.

6. Then go back and complete all missing thoughts, quotes, phrases that will strengthen your paper, and again don't stop.

7. Re-read the paper and complete a final edit to errors, phrasing and misspelled words.

8. Allow a colleague, friend or mentor to read through your paper from beginning to end to give any final corrections.

There you have it!

The enemy to this concept of "distraction free speed writing" is trying to edit and correct spelling mistakes as you go. The second enemy is trying to multi-task or do other things while you are writing your paper.

Uninterrupted focus is essential!

As I mentioned earlier, there is DISTRACTION FREE computer software that will assist in this. This software will help you focus on writing by "blacking out" your screen, except the document area in which you are writing.

Here are a few suggestions:
- Write Room (Mac-Only)
- JDarkRoom
- q10 (PC-only)
- Writer (online application)

So do you understand this simple concept?

If you are so bold, you can even dim the light on your computer screen and type without looking at what is being etched out. So can you do this? Can you make this happen to speed up your writing?

Well, there's my advice on how to make this happen.

If you have other suggestions, I would love for you to send me your suggestions and leave your thoughts and advise in the form of an email to *Kantis@PlayingYourAGame.com*

As a sophomore in college at Norfolk State University, I set out to get my very first 4.0 as a college student. In doing so, I set certain boundaries and disciplines for myself. A few of them I want to definitely share with you today.

1. I chose **to study, learn, and associate with 4.0 students.** I figured that if I wanted to be "great" then I had to hang with "great" students.

2. I also chose to **use my time better and maximize my daily progress** by maximizing every single hour of the day.

3. Lastly I **learned how to get in the bed** and go to sleep. Yes, sleep helped me get a 4.0.

Why Sleep Is Essential to Your Academic Success

You probably know that you need a full 7-8 hours of sleep at night in order to perform at your very best, but most grown-ups in North America don't get that much. Are you getting all the zzz's that you need? Chances are that you're not. You know it's important, but you're busy, you have so much to study and learn, you have other responsibilities, and sleep is the first thing to go, right?

The problem with that is that lack of sleep can be downright harmful and incapacitating. And when you're sleep-deprived, it may be hard to use your normal good judgment to know how essential sleep really is. So, here is a reminder of why sleep is so essential to your academic success and the great benefits of getting your rest:

1. You need a full 7-8 consecutive hours of good sleep in order to wake up refreshed and full of energy. When you are refreshed and full of energy your tasks seem easier. You feel good, and strong. You feel capable. When you feel this way you can accomplish much more and you can do it in a shorter amount of time.

2. Getting enough sleep makes your brain work better and makes you better able to think. Your mind is clear and sharp after a good night's sleep.

You understand things more quickly, and you are much more effective at problem solving.

3. You need sleep to create important memory links and connections. When you first learn something that information is fragile, the imprint on your brain is very delicate. When you sleep your brain reviews that information and forges stronger pathways so it becomes a more solid part of your knowledge base. And we all know how very important a good memory is to your academic success!

4. Sleep boosts your immunity. You need sleep to keep your body healthy. Have you ever noticed how easy it is to catch colds when you aren't getting enough sleep and you let your body's resistance go down? And how effectively do you study and learn when you have a case of the sniffles?

5. Lack of sleep makes you feel crummy. Lack of sleep creates unpleasant states such as increased stress, fatigue -- where your whole body aches all over, drowsiness -- so you feel sleepy even though it is daytime. Obviously, these are not ideal states for your academic success.

There you have it. Sleep is a powerful tool to help you reach the levels of academic success you are striving for. Keep up the good work, focus and remove the distractions, and when it's time to get some sleep - GET SOME ZZZZZZZZZ.

A FOCUSED GAMEPLAN
Take the time to think, answer, and take action now

Who or what is a distraction in your life?

_____
_____
_____
_____
_____
_____
_____
_____
_____

What can you practically do to remove the distraction?

_____
_____
_____
_____
_____
_____
_____
_____
_____
_____
_____
_____
_____
_____
_____

Write about four areas you decide to be more focused in.

_____

_____

_____

_____

_____

_____

_____

_____

_____

_____

Detail the practical steps you will take to accomplish that focus in those four areas.

_____

_____

_____

_____

_____

_____

_____

_____

_____

_____

_____

play #6

Get Your Game Up

Academic Success Skills - What are they and how do you develop them?

Well these are the basic skills that every student, regardless of grade, degree level, or area of study must develop. Just like there are skills that a carpenter or doctor must have, academic success skills are the foundation skills for every student to make learning more efficient and more rewarding. Students who know and use these skills get better scores on exams, enjoy the "student life", and experience longevity in their academic pursuit.

As a high school student, traditional college student or adult student, your success depends on these. Understanding and developing these Academic Success Skill is an investment for your today and your tomorrow. Every student must:

1. Learn How to Listen Carefully

On my website I wrote a blog post, "*7.25 Academic Survival Skills that Every Student Must Develop*", where we detailed each of the survival skills that you must develop to be a successful student. Those blog post were great online, so I'm going to address them here in this chapter as well.

The first academic survival skill – **LISTENING**!

If you think about most of your day as a student, the

majority of your time is spent listening to your professor lecture. So if you are taking 15 credits of college courses, this tells me you are spending a minimum of 15 hours a week consistently listening. As a high school student, at least 6 hours of the day is spent in the classroom listening to teachers or participating in class discussions; which equates to about 30 hours of classroom listening.

So as you see, if we are going to spend most of our week listening, it is essential to become an active listener.

Here are a few things you can do to improve your classroom listening skills as a high school student, college student or non-traditional student.

1. Come to class well rested and energized. Your sleep is very   important to your grades.

2. Be prepared for class. Come prepared by completing any and all previous reading assignments or homework. It's always best to be ahead of the teacher's syllabus.

3. Move to the front or "energy zone" of the professor. This is the part of the classroom, where the professor focuses most of his speaking energy when he speaks. This normally is the area, where students are giving the professor the most attention. Also move closer to the front so you won't have any

trouble seeing, hearing or paying attention.

4. Focus your attention on what the speaker is saying – not on the upcoming weekend, the sound of the speaker's voice, or any thing else that doesn't matter.

5. Evaluate what you hear – think about what the professor's or teacher's words mean and how they relate to what you already know about the class subject.

6. Take great notes. Since it's impossible for even the best listeners to remember all that has been said, take great notes.

So now you have six ways you can apply to improve your classroom listening skills. Since your academic success relies on listening, begin today putting these simple techniques together. I would also like to hear other ways you have improved your listening and retained classroom information. Send me an email at Kantis@PlayingYourAGame.com with your technique and strategy.

2. Develop a Note-Taking System.

While sitting in a class listening, the better you take and write your notes, the better your chances will be during your personal study sessions and how you perform on test and exams.

When was the last time you asked for someone's phone number, and realized later that you were missing one of the digits? Did you go into stalker mode, and replace that missing digit by calling the number with a 0, then a 1, then a 2... 3....4.....5.......9, until you got the appropriate person on the other line?

Taking notes in the classroom is similar to writing down an important phone number; if you don't get all the digits, you will be unable to speak with the person you desire to talk to. The same is true when you don't get the most important information during your class by taking good notes; when it's time to study for your test or exam you will be unequipped with the information for the next test or quiz.

To better assist you with note-taking, I want to detail "WHAT" to record and "HOW" to record it when taking notes during class.

HERE'S WHAT TO RECORD

* Record the most important information (just like the most important digits of a phone number). Don't try to write verbatim everything the teacher says, but jot down the main points in your OWN words.

* Listen for the key words that indicate what's important. Phrases like... "The major cause was...", "This is something you should remember," etc.

126

* Copy all important charts, sentences, and phrases that were posted on the board by the teacher. That way you have something to refer back to when studying.

HERE'S HOW TO RECORD IT

* Utilize symbols and abbreviations when taking notes. Try to use a few words as possible.

* Only use half of the paper (left or right) when taking notes in class. Utilize the other side (right or left) to come up with potential test questions and other notes that will support the study notes you took in class.

• Use the outline format if possible when taking notes. It helps you give a systematic order to your notes. It also helps you retain it better, because of the viewable order.

Lastly, it is imperative that you attend class if you are going to take good notes. If you are going to take good notes, it is imperative that you review your notes immediately and regularly. This second survival skill along with the other Academic Survival skills will definitely set you on course to play your "A" game.

3. Learn How to Actively Participate In Class

It is a huge plus when you can participate in class discussions. It's imperative that you take advantage of the opportunity to express your opinions and test the ideas you gather in class. It also impresses your teachers and/or professors.

Have you ever been called or known as the "teacher's pet?"

Been accused of "brown nosing" the teacher?

What about "kissing up?"

How about trying to "Suck up" or "Get in good" with your professor or teacher?

Don't confuse these terms with someone who accurately participates in class for the purpose of improving their grades and understanding of the subject. There is a difference – one seeks the favor of the teacher, while the other is after the content being offered.

Just recently while speaking at a high-school, I had a conversation with a student and he asked me the following question:

"Kantis, how can I better participate in class? For a percentage of our overall final class score is based on class participation. Yet I don't really know what to say

in class because I don't want to seem stupid in front of my classmates. Plus, I'm very very shy. What can I do about this?"

As I began to have a few words with this young man in the lobby of the auditorium, I proceeded to let him know that active class participation is a great way to enhance what you are learning in the classroom through open discussion. It also gives your teacher a clear viewpoint that you are seriously trying to ace his or her class.

Here are the few things I recommended to the student for effective class participation and I recommend them to you as well.

> * **Come prepared to class** – this is done by always being ahead of your teacher where class "reading" is concerned, completion of all home work problems or given assignments and the updating of all your class notes. Those three things will prepare you for every class session.

> • **Ask clear questions** – if you are confused about anything, don't hesitate to ask clear questions that help remove any mental blockage. This is also one of the best ways to learn; so ask questions.

> * **Verbally summarize what has been previously said** – This will ensure that you understand what someone else has said or what your teacher has said.

* **Participate and don't dominate** – don't be too active in class by having all the attention on your questions and comments. Knowing when to listen is just as important as knowing when to speak.

* **Always respect your other classmates' opinion.** Be open to their comments or questions if you disagree with them or have a difference of opinion, and be open to what others have to say. You could learn a lot for others

* **Be respectful and courteous** – if you don't want it done to you, don't do it to others. This is the Golden Rule for class participation. Just be courteous!

I believe participating in class is another Academic Survival Skill that every student should develop.

4. Learn How to Budget Your Time

You have a set number of hours in the classroom, a set number of hours needed for studying, and other set hours for resting, eating, sleeping, working and enjoying life. How you mange, use, budget, or abuse this precious time will also determine your academic success or the lack thereof.

As a student, you only have 24 hours in a day, which mean 168 hours in a week.

Most high school students are in the classroom 6-8 hours a day.

Most college students are in the classroom, 15 hours a week.

Non-traditional students spend about 6 hours a week taking classes in addition to working a 40 hour work week.

Regardless of what level you are currently in, we only get 24 hours during the day.

> *"I Need More Time!"*
> *"I just don't have enough time."*
> *"I wish I didn't have so much to do."*
> *"If there were only more days in a week."*
> *"I'm so busy; I wish there were two of me."*
> *"So much to do, so little time."*

And the list can go on and on.

You've heard these comments before. In fact, you've probably used a couple of them yourself from time to time (excuse the pun). But one of the biggest lies we tell almost every single day (and people seem to believe) is "I don't have enough time." If you think I'm being a little hard on you, well I am, but no harder than I am on myself. Below I have attached some key essentials in optimizing your 24's!

1. Schedule quiet, motivational time. See your day in your head before the actual day.

2. Allocate the times you must be in class.

3. Define the time periods in which you will study.

4. Plan for breakfast and lunch, but don't eat for longer than 30 minutes, use the other designated half hour to prepare for next class.

5. Set time aside for part time jobs, extracurricular activities, and other necessary events.

6. Carry a detailed appointment book or organizer, so you will always know what needs to be done for the day.

7. Communicate your study times to friends and family, so they are aware of your schedule and won't interfere.

5. Become a Great Reader

Researchers have shown that people who read well are more likely to do well academically. So it's wise to bury bad habits while developing the good habits of effective reading. Have you ever heard the powerful phrase, *"Readers are leaders and leaders are leaders"*?

What about this one, *"Rich people read books, and poor people watch TV"?*

Well whatever you have heard about reading, one thing is for sure, people who read well are more likely to do well academically.

I remember growing up as a student, and I hated to read books because it seemed like a long process or it seemed like the prelude before sleep. I even remember reading Cliff Notes, and the beginning and ends of chapters of books just to TRY to get an advantage over reading the entire text. But after three college degrees, I saw the direct correlation between my poor test grades and my reading efforts. I was always under prepared when I did not FULLY and EFFECTIVELY read.

Maybe you are currently (like I use to be) dreading to read? Heres a few things you can do develop this fifth academic survival skill called READING.

Eliminate Bad Reading Habits

Starting today, eliminate the following bad habits that slow you down when you are reading a book, article, paper or journal entry.

* Don't move your lips while you are reading, but "SAY" your words in your mind, or use your finger as a fluid pointer.

* Train your eyes to take in large group of words, at every glance – not just one word in each sentence.

* Avoid backtracking. Stop rereading the same sentence that you keep reading over and over again. Keep it moving.

Adjust Your Speed

According to what you are reading, and the purpose of the material you are reading, adjust your speed of reading accordingly. Here are a few examples:

* Skim the material if you are looking for the answer to a particular question.

* Slow down when you are reading technical subjects, like equations, science or math.

Expand Your Vocabulary

If at all possible, strive to expand your vocabulary when you read.

* I suggest using a dictionary, or web program that will easily help you learn the definition, synonyms and antonyms of new words.

* Understand what certain prefixes, suffixes, and roots of words mean. You can find books in the library or search the web for resources to help you.

* When given the opportunity, use the new words

that you learn in your everyday speech. It will help your vocabulary as well, just make sure you really know the full definition of the word. I try to do this a lot in my speeches.

Get Help When You Need It

If you are having challenges in reading:

* Enroll in a reading class. It's okay! It's actually a cool thing to read.

* Check with your school or university to see if they may have some helpful speed reading courses.

Okay, here is my challenge to you. Better your reading skills by reading on a daily basis.

What books you are currently reading? What are the last three books you have read or are in the process of reading?

Besides reading my book, here are some other books that I recommend for personal development:

• *Teens Guide to World Domination, by Josh Shipp*

• *Love is Greater than Hate, by Brooks Gibbs*

• *You Were Born An Original, Don't Live Like a Copy, by Jonathan Sprinkles*

• *I Went to College, and I Don't Know Why? by Kantis Simmons*

6. Perfect Your Study Strategy

This skill may be the one skill that sets "A" students apart from average students. What you do before classes, during classes, and after classes contributes greatly to how you learn, understand and apply the concepts of the subjects you are learning.

Every Sunday in the fall I normally do two things – go to church and watch NFL Football.

One thing that is apparent about every football game is that both teams come with a STRATEGY to beat their opponent. The determination of the winner is based solely on who carried out their strategy with the least amount of mistakes.

When it comes to academic success, preparing for tests, and succeeding as a high school or college student; STUDYING is a major skill you must develop. This skill will definitely help your daily regimen. Here are some simple guidelines you can use to improve your reading-studying strategy, as well as make the most of your time spent studying.

Before You Read
Before you read the next assignment for your class from the textbook, make sure you do the following:

- READ the chapter title and introductions.
- READ all subheadings and topic sentences.

• READ the bold face words and italicized words.
• READ the chapter summary and any review questions.

As Your Read

During your study time, as you are reading the text or chapter, make sure you add these to your strategy:

• Pay attention to all main ideas and supporting details.
• Pay attention to graphs, charts, or any illustrations.
• Pay attention to what you read. Evaluate the content. Do you agree with it? Does the material answer the questions about the subject?

After Your Read

Once you have completed your reading and applied the strategies above:

• Think about what you've learned. And verbally (speak aloud) summarize the content of the material. This will improve your retention.
• Identify and note points you don't fully understand so that you can bring those questions up in class to your professor or instructor.

Having a study strategy is key to winning and playing your "A" game in the classroom. Some other things you can do to improve your study strategy is to change some bad habits you are currently doing, improve you memory retention techniques, and get better sleep.

Having these study skills and more like it will definitely improve the grades you are currently getting.

7. Learn How to Prepare for Exams

When you are PREPARED for testing OPPORTUNI-TIES success is inevitable; however, if you don't know how to review your notes, communicate the concepts of the subject and solve problems on exams, you can stunt your growth as a successful student.

Taking tests, preparing for exams, studying for mid-terms, and studying for final exams traditionally give students challenges. With so many things taking place before test time, there seems to be a rush of adrena-line to the mind containing fear, stress, overload and anxiety. I have experienced these same symptoms be-fore test time, until I learned a few key ways to prepare for test.

Understanding how to prepare for tests or exams is a vital academic skill that every student must develop.

Yes, reviewing your class notes regularly can make studying for exams easier and more efficient, but here are some other key ways that you can prepare for those exams. These may seem easy and simple, but they are very effective.

Here are 7.25 Ways to Prepare for Tests

1. ASK THE INSTRUCTOR – When was the last time you just walked into your teacher's office and asked, *"Excuse me instructor. What shall I expect on the test? What material will be covered? Will the test be essay or objective? What should I concentrate on when preparing?"* Now what is the worst thing the teacher can say? NO, I'm not telling?

2. LOOK UP PAST COPIES – I can assure you that what you are being tested on is not the first time it is in exam form. So check with your library or older students to see if old exams are available. This can give you a general idea what to expect on the test. Please don't rely heavily on this; it's only for your preparation.

3. MAKE YOUR OWN TEST – From everything your instructor has talked about, put yourself in the shoes of your instructor and make up your OWN test. Put down on paper ten good questions you think would be great test questions, and answer them.

4. REVIEW YOUR NOTES – Go over and reread all highlighted sections of your text again. Don't re-read the entire text, just highlighted areas that are also in your notes. If possible, make up test questions from these highlighted notes as mentioned above. If you are still having challenges taking good notes, then review the academic survival skill on note-taking.

5. CALL A STUDY GROUP – Have a true "TEST PARTY". Gather no more than 5 people, and form a circle. Taking turns, have each person ask a potential test question to one person in the circle. This will help you prepare your answers, and see how others answered the questions in the game. At the end of the game, discuss among your classmates all the correct answers and why.

6. GET A GOOD NIGHT SLEEP – Sleeping is so amazing. It refreshes the body and refreshes your mind to think strong and clearly. In a blog post on "Sleeping your Way to better grades," I go into more detail as to why sleep is so important to your academic success.

7. EAT LIGHTLY – This is really simple, but very necessary. Don't bog your tummy down with greasy foods, this is equivalent to putting dirty gas in your car. Get it? Instead eat something in the morning that is living (i.e. fruits, vegetables, pure juices). This will help get your "test motor" running.

7.25 HAVE A WINNING ATTITUDE – This alone has caused so many people to fail that I must address it. However you envision yourself, that will you be. If your inner voice is saying you will fail or that you are not prepared – then in most cases, YOU will. As a cheerleader is to a football team, you must be to your inner mindset and attitude. After preparing and properly studying for an exam, cheer yourself up and tell yourself that you can play your "A" game and ace this exam.

Well, there it is! Some simple things you can do to pass those exams and tests. I would love to hear how you have done. Send me an email and let me know how things have been going for you on your tests.

I would love to hear from you. You can send your email to Kantis@PlayingYourAGame.com

Build Your Study Chamber

Above, we discussed the Academic Success Skills that every student must develop. But don't you realize that these skills won't do you any good if the atmosphere for studying isn't correct?

Now let's think for a second... Where are you currently studying? What places do you study and get the most out of your study time?

Some people study at the kitchen table. Some people study in the library, and some study in their bedroom, office, or common area.

Regardless of where you are currently studying, I advise that you build a personal study chamber.

Now would it be appropriate to eat my dinner sitting in the bathroom on the toilet? (Too vivid right?)

Would it be correct for me to take a bath in the kitchen

sink?

How about bring the lawn mower in the living room to clean the carpet? Just as weird as these scenarios sound, it is also weird for you to study your class work in a place that is not suitable for studying.

Just like the bathroom has a purpose, the kitchen has a purpose, and the bedroom has a purpose, your study chamber has a purpose - studying.

As a Academic Success Coach, there are many things I love to do that do not pertain to academics. When I am not speaking or traveling to schools I love to kick back and watch shows on Home and Garden Television (HGTV). "Design on a Dime", "Designer's Challenge", and "Divine Design" are few of my favorite TV shows. They all fuel my hobby of home decor and home decorating.

So let me take my home decor hobby plus my academic success wits and help you build and decorate your personal study chamber or study location.

• Establish a place to study outside of your bedroom.

• Study in a clean and organized environment.

• Keep your study location cool. Warm rooms = sluggishness. Cool rooms = alertness

• Study in well lit conditions. You must be able to SEE it if you will ever be able to LEARN it. Plus, poorly lit rooms can stress and will damage your eyes when reading.

• Avoid studying in the bed - you WILL eventually fall asleep.

• Choose a location where a telephone is not accessible. If that's not possible, allow voicemail to work for you. "I am studying, please call after..."

• Make sure a television isn't in operation near your location. You can't concentrate on two things. You are not that smart.

• Avoid studying in high-traffic study areas, so you won't get distracted.

Hopefully, you can get creative in building your customized study location. If it's real nice maybe we can both go on a HGTV reality show to feature your study location.

Let's Talk About CRAMMING

If I could show you how to C.R.A.M. your way into better grades, would you do it? Would you look at cramming differently?

Now you are probably thinking, *"Cramming isn't that successful. I can't cram my way to a 4.0."* Your thoughts are valid but I want to propel your life as a student and as an individual by bringing you to a higher level of thinking. You're probably very familiar with cramming. Most students do it, stay up late the night before a big test and cram as much information into your brain at the last minute. A couple things to consider about this type of cramming:

1) it hardly ever works and
2) it doesn't work at the last minute.

BUT, if used at the proper time, C.R.A.M.ming can bring forth great results. Take this example from my college years.

As a Freshman Chemistry major at Norfolk State University, I made some bad academic decisions. I was a P.P. – a Professional Procrastinator. I would wait until the last minute to do everything. I waited until the last minute to study notes, prepare for tests, work on homework and finish reports. I procrastinated so much; I waited until the last minute to go to the cafeteria to eat. This last minute lifestyle forced me to have many cram sessions, pull all-nighters and sometimes miss meals.

Since I was on an academic scholarship, I realized in order to maintain my scholarship and graduate with honors, my poor study habits and lack of time management was going to have to change. This became further apparent when I had to repeat exams with headaches and aching body pains.

During the exam, I would feel sluggish and crappy; like I had a serious hangover. I actually did - a hangover from the previous night of cramming, drinking bottles of root beer, eating candy bars and greasy pizza all for the sake of trying to stay awake to focus.

Reports have shown that cramming or "last-minute studying" causes unhealthy symptoms. If you are a consistent crammer, you can testify to the following:

- Your anxiety level increases tremendously.

- You lose sleep and eat poorly.

- You are susceptible to illness and sicknesses.

- You are tardy or even miss the exam time.

- You take the more difficult essay make-up exam, because you missed the original exam.

- You simply fail the exam.

- You perform worse on the exam than you would have otherwise. Guaranteed.

Last minute cramming does not work because of a few biological reasons.

When cramming occurs, information is stored in the short-term memory side of the brain. This is where everyday information that is not really worth remembering is stored. In order to learn we have to transfer information into the long-term memory side of the brain. Here information can be retrieved far easier and is stored over a longer period of time. Let's further examine the difference between short-term and long-term memory.

All information is processed in the brain and stored in short term memory. When the short-term memory overloads the braid with information, you can start to forget it.

Can you remember what you had for breakfast two days ago, or the outfit you wore this past weekend?

What about the price of your lunch on Monday? No?

Long term memory is the type of memory used when we want to store information in a more permanent way. This is either done by making information especially memorable or by consistent repetition.

Have you ever tried to remember the lyrics to your favorite song? How many times did you listen to that song or read the lyrics before you finally remembered it? The same should be true for your class work. Once something is transferred from short term to long term memory we successfully say it has been learned, or at least remembered.

So with understanding long-term and short-term memory, you understand why cramming is pointless, it will always leave you coming up short.

C.R.A.M. as I have termed, can be translated into a simple four-word phrase – Consistent Reiteration for Advantageous Memorization. It is imperative that you study your class work (C.R.A.M) every single day, even if it is only for a few minutes.

Your current occupation is a "student" and you will have this job title until you graduate; so see school as your 9 to 5 job. When it's time to study a class subject, work just as if it were your full-time job, making sure you check-in and out at a certain time each day. You should have daily C.R.A.M. sessions throughout the school term so the information can transfer to long-term memory.

My main reason for addressing this issue of cramming versus C.R.A.M.ming, is to impress upon you to develop DAILY DISCIPLINES. The thing you give your attention to the most, will be the thing that controls your mindset and memory bank.

You have what it takes to play your "A" game every school term. Just don't wait until the last minute to cram, but C.R.A.M. every single day with a planned regimen.

Many students fail because they fail to plan. To better your grades, you must have a detailed plan of attack and mastery over your daily schedule.

7.25 Vital Reasons to C.R.A.M. as a student:

1. You will be better prepared for quizzes, tests and exams.

2. You will retain more information to use later rather than learning it for a test, then forgetting it.

3. You will rest and sleep better.

4. You will be more confident and less anxious about exams, tests or quizzes.

5. You will be healthier, and more focused and alert during the exam.

6. You will not have to repeat the exam, or take that silly essay makeup exam.

7. You will become the student others want to study with because you know the class material.

7.25 You will have better grades and a great GPA.

Here Are Some DO-DO's for Studying

DO-DO's

- Prioritize your study time, study the challenging subjects first.

- Identify when and where you will study, and with whom (if needed).

- Study continually throughout the semester not just before a test.

- Study in a clean and organized environment.

- Keep your notebooks and notes organized; it will help when needing to refer back.

- Drink plenty of water.

- Keep your room cool. Warm rooms = sluggishness. Cool rooms = alertness (that's why movie theatres are so chilly).

- Study in well lit conditions.

- Set goals and timetables for your study sessions.

- Be aggressive and proactive about your study time.

- Guard and protect your study time, by staying focused.

- Take a five-minute break every 55 minutes, and then resume studying.

149

DON'T - DOs

- Avoid studying in the bed - you WILL eventually fall asleep.

- Avoid studying while on the phone; let voicemail work for you. "I am studying, please call after..."

- Turn off the TV; you can't concentrate on two things. You are not that smart.

- Turn off that hip-hop/rock/rap music; if anything, use soft classical, slow jazz, or earth tones.

- Avoid studying after eating greasy or heavy meals.

- Avoid drinks with caffeine or lots of sugar; they will eventually make you sluggish.

- Avoid studying in high-traffic study areas , so you won't get distracted by your friends or those of the opposite sex.

- Avoid studying with those whom you have a "crush" on or physically attracted to. I guess you know what will eventually happen.

- Avoid trying to study while text messaging, chatting on the internet or responding to email.

So there you have it, Play #6 is to get your skills up. Develop all the key skills to become a success inside and outside the classroom.

play #7

Stop the Stress
Test Mess

Overcoming Test Anxiety

In this part of Playing Your "A" Game, we will discuss and share the symptoms of test anxiety and the one question to ask yourself when dealing with it; and how to overcome it so it never invades your thinking again. So many students deal with this on school tests, and final exams; both in high school and in college. Your academic success in education is solely based on how you approach all of your exams.

WHAT IS TEST ANXIETY?

Test Anxiety is all the positive and/or negative feelings that consume your thinking, emotions, and actions before, during and after taking school exams, quizzes, and important tests. What does it feel like?

It feels like:

- pressure
- stress
- headache
- being overwhelmed
- uncertainty
- nervousness
- anxiousness
- confusion
- gas
- excitement

Silly But Real Symptoms Of Test Anxiety

Here are some indicators and patterns to clearly determine if you experience test anxiety. Answer "yes" to the symptoms that most (closely) apply to you:

- You have trouble sleeping at night and spend those last few minutes before sleep worrying about upcoming exams or projects.

- The day of an exam, You experience drastic appetite changes and either overeat, or skip breakfast and lunch.

- While studying for or taking an exam, You often feel a sense of hopelessness or dread.

- You often yawn during an exam or while studying.

- While studying or taking an exam, you have problems concentrating and you sometimes feel bored or tired.

- During an exam, you often feel confused or panic.

- During an exam, you experience sweaty palms, and/or mental blocks.

- While taking an exam, you sometimes experience headaches, vomiting, or fainting.

• After the exam, you pretend the exam meant nothing to you, and discard the result as meaningless.

• When finished with your exam, you sometimes feel guilt and blame yourself for not studying enough. "My Fault"!

• As a general rule, you view test taking as a stressful situation and dread it.

If you answered YES to any of the above then you battle with test anxiety.

To better explain how to deal with test anxiety and all the pains, symptoms and setbacks, I want to make reference to a mp3 player.

As you know an mp3 player is an audio device that plays music on it. You can store audio files on it and play it as you desire through headphones.

My current mp3 player is an Apple iPod; which has approximately 2539 audio files on it. Some of the files contain music, some of the files are audio books, some of the files are podcasts, and some of the files are seminars.

My iPod gives me the unique ability to repeat certain audio files over and over. I can listen to one music track on my iPod all day long if I desired to. It will play continuously until 1) the battery runs out, 2) I stop the track or 3) I change the track.

The best way to deal with text anxiety is the same way you deal with an iPod that continually plays the same song over and over again. You change the track!

When was the last time, your internal mental iPod played negative thoughts on your mind? When was the last time you sat down to take a test, and you heard the negative statements...You can't pass. You won't pass. You will fail.

Don't allow negative thoughts, images, words, phrases, and fears to control your thinking before during or after the test.

To overcome this you must:

- **Refuel your mind with positive thoughts.**

- **Demolish the ability of negative thoughts to reside and abide in your thinking.**

- **Openly confess to yourself that you can succeed and will succeed.**

Change the track, and play a new track. Stop the stress test mess and begin to prepare, prepare and prepare. Be well equipped for every quiz, test, and exam.

"When opportunity meets preparation, success is inevitable."

** Make sure you review those test taking tips I gave you a few chapters back, so you will be prepared for every test**

Cheaters are Wimpers – Honor the Honor Code!

The other day, one of my best friends called me and updated me on her most recent final exams. She told me how well she did, and how she had been applying the tips and tricks she learned to play her "A" Game. She was so excited that she now believes she will be getting an "A" in that college class.

Then with disgust, she mentions that while she was taking her test she heard two students talking during her final exams. She looked at them, but could not understand a word they were saying - they were speaking in another language.

As she sat there, another student too witnessed these two men talking during the final exams. What were they talking about at this crucial time? They were cheating!

Should they turn these students in or should they let this pass?

157

"Tell or don't tell? That is the question!

In my first year at Georgia Institute of Technology, I came to better understand the importance of honor. There was a situation that took place during my first semester that I had never experienced before. I was taking an engineering test in a class made up primarily of international students. The professor was not present. During the exam, I heard a foreign language being spoken in the classroom. To this day, I have no idea what was said, but I know there should not have been any talking during the test. I assumed that a few students were cheating, but I blocked the thought out of my head. Unfortunately it happened again during another test, except this time I heard papers being passed around. Despite the evidence, I again let the situation slide.

When it happened a third time, I wrote an unsigned letter to the department head and to all the professors of the classes in which I believed the students were cheating. In my letter I expressed my observations during each test session. I specifically mentioned each instance I felt the students were cheating. I expressed my belief that these actions were unfair to other students and that a flagrant violation to the honor code took place that required an investigation and possible disciplinary action.

After a few days, the professor returned the exams and made a public comment about the letter in which I had

158

written. He went on to express that the institution held the Honor Code in the highest regard and required that all students abide by it. In addition, the professor stated that students who were witnesses to cheating were required to report what they had observed.

I knew about the first part of the code, but not the latter. The professor suggested that the "disturbed graduate student" come and see him to discuss the matter personally with him; thereafter, he would investigate the situation. I met with him after class in his office, and he explained to me my part of the honor code; to report violations by confronting the student personally or informing the professor of the alleged infraction. When he had finished speaking, I told him of my observations.

After two semesters of investigating and keeping a thorough watch on the alleged violators, these students were caught red-handed. The professors finally realized that what I had observed and reported was obviously true.

Is cheating something that you witness, but don't say anything about? Do you let it pass like so many others do? I encourage you to walk in honor, even if situational ethics say it is okay to "sneak a peek" or plagiarize something.

Honor is doing what's right when no one is looking. Honor is directly related to one's character. It defines who you are, when you are all alone without any class-mates or supervision. So what does your character say about you? Are you the student that occasionally goes the extra mile to get the answers for the test from your peers? Or are you the student that spends time writing the answers to the exam on the palm of your hand? Maybe you are the "techie" cheater, who knows how to program the answers and study notes in your cell phone or scientific calculator? If you are one of the above, I encourage you today to cut the nonsense out. Stop living a dishonorable life, and make a decision today to walk in integrity. "God don't like ugly" is what my elders use to say.

My friend did the honorable thing. She notified her teacher by writing a huge note to her professor ON HER EXAM.

So what will you do? Tell or don't tell?

THE GAMEPLAN FOR
TEST SUCCESS

Take the time to think, answer, and take action now.

What few things do you say to yourself days before a test?

_____

_____

_____

_____

_____

_____

_____

_____

_____

What few things do you say to yourself right before a test?

_____

_____

_____

_____

_____

_____

_____

_____

_____

_____

Playing Your A Game

What do you say to yourself while taking the test?

_____
_____
_____
_____
_____
_____
_____
_____
_____
_____
_____

Where did these negative thoughts come from? Where in the past were you disappointed?

_____
_____
_____
_____
_____
_____
_____
_____
_____
_____
_____
_____
_____
_____

Determine now, that your past failures won't hinder your future. Jot down a statement of confidence with some strong positive words to secure your future (write in the space below).

_____

_____

_____

_____

_____

_____

_____

_____

_____

_____

_____

_____

_____

_____

_____

_____

_____

_____

_____

_____

_____

_____

_____

_____

_____

_____

play #7.25

Set Your Habits and Leave Them There

After 30 something years of living on this earth, I am finally admitting I have a problem. I've battled with this problem for many years. My parents have tried to help me and so has my wife but today the buck stops here.

Before you judge me and before I reveal to you my bad habit, let's talk about STUDY HABITS.

As a student, what study habits have you developed? Do you study in bed?

Do you spend time looking at each subject every day?

Do you find yourself distracted when you study?

Whatever the case, always keep in mind…

The Study Habits you develop will determine your academic success; so establish GOOD study habits and respect those habits.

Here's my coming out: I bite my finger nails.

For years, I have looked at my hands, put my fingers in my mouth and chewed on whatever nail was long enough to fit in between my teeth. Don't get me wrong, I haven't bitten them down to the bone, I do have some nail to work with, but I have developed a habit of biting my nails. But today I have decided to change this habit and respect this new habit.

You might say Kantis, I need to change some study habits. Well take a look at these tips below to initiate the new habits you want to develop,

1. Make a quality decision to change.

2. Become accountable to someone and set boundaries to protect your decision.

3. Develop new and good habits. Apply the "Do-Do's of Studying."

Changing some of your study habits will change how you perform academically. Once you begin to implement your new habits you must set up boundaries that will protect you from returning to the old habits.

In order for me to be successful in my new habit of not biting my finger nails, I have created the boundaries of keeping my fingers away from my mouth unless I am eating, consistently getting manicures and paying a ten dollar fine to my wife whenever I break my new habit. I will create a new habit of not biting my nails and I will respect that habit or my wife will be very rich.

Developing good study habits will help you academically achieve success in all your classes.

Simple Must-Have Academic Habits

To achieve all the success you desire in this school year, I have laid out some simple habits that I encourage all students to develop. Before we jump right in, let's define what a "HABIT" is. Habit - an acquired behavior pattern regularly followed until it has become almost involuntary; something you do automatically without thinking. It's your particular practice or usage. Here are some great examples:

• Saying "Good morning" to the first few people you greet

• Looking both ways before you cross the street

• Biting your finger nails

• Flipping the light switch on when you walk in a dark room

Below, I have outlined some key habits that will set you up for winning in school. Take the time to look at each of them. Develop a plan to tackle them one by one. If you can't develop all of them at once, then choose one to work on every week.

As you begin to look at each of these Academic habits, take some time to think about other bad habits that may be hindering your success in school.

Academic Habits for School Success
Dreams don't come true – Goals do. Before next summer rolls around again, what academic goals do you want to achieve?

• Draft up your Goals.
Set academic goals to achieve, write them down and post them in a place where you can look at them everyday. You should first sit down with your family and discuss the desired goal and then set your academic goals. Make those goals positive, personal, and in the present. Then, write down your goals and make them visible in four key places: (1) the bedroom, (2) the bathroom, (3) the kitchen, and (4) in your notebooks.

• Develop your Plan.
ow that you have determined your goals you must develop a plan to achieve them. Come up with a systematic routine that you can follow every day to achieve your goals and write it down. Set aside time for necessities like breakfast, dinner, fun, chores, sleeping, socializing and of course study time. Remember, when you fail to plan, you plan to fail.

• Draw from your Super Powers.
Identify the period of day when you are most alert or "wired up" outside of school. This should be the time YOU study. Traditionally, the pattern for *study time* has been right after you get home and change out of your school clothes or right before dinner time.

(Remember school clothes, church clothes, and play clothes?). After spending 6-9 hours in school, it may be wise to incorporate nap-time or refresher-time before studying. Studies have shown that students perform poorly when they are mentally tired, drained or unfocused. Whatever time you are most alert outside of school, make that your study time. I guarantee you will see an increase in academic performance.

• Develop your Family Connection.
Make sure you have weekly family chat sessions or what I like to call Family Love Sessions. Take this time to discuss school crushes, fashion trends, music, insecurities, and future plans. Family is a key element to achieving your goals because they will assist you when you need it. This is also a great time to develop better relationships. (An alternative to this is setting time with a mature friend, mentor or adviser).

• Destroy the TV.
You should already know that television can steal your time and productivity. You do not have to stop watching television in order to achieve your academic goals but watching during your peak performance time can hinder your progress. So brush the dust off your VCR or learn how to use a DVR and watch your favorite shows during your non-peak performing times. Use all the new technology to your benefit and don't ever allow television to steal the precious hours you have available during the day.

• Dwell in the Zone.

The kitchen has a specific purpose, the bathroom has a specific purpose, and your study chamber has a specific purpose. You should not eat dinner in the bathroom and you should not shower in the kitchen. There are also things you should not do in your study chamber. Your study chamber should be a specific location where only one thing happens – STUDYING.

• Defeat Fear.

Believe it or not, FEAR is the one thing that can destroy academic performance. Most term it "anxiety" and as a student you experience it during tests, when you are embarrassed around your classmates or when you feel unprepared. Despite setting goals and studying, FEAR can completely destroy your efforts. It can also cause you to become unfocused and think that you will fail and not reach your goals. Always remember this, *FEAR is False Evidence Appearing Real* – FEAR is not real. Whenever you experience anxiety or may be fearful, remember you do not have to be, because failure is only appearing to be real, it is fake. Therefore, in school or in life, never FEAR!

• Declare Your Greatness.

Your mouth has the power to create so establish positive confessions and declare them out loud daily. Since our words frame how we think and feel, say only the best. Don't commit "goal suicide" by speaking negative words, thinking negative thoughts, and having negative feelings. Talk your way to achieving your goals.

Study Class Subjects Every Day, Even When You Don't Have Class

Have you ever heard the phrase, "What you put in, is what you will get out?" Well this phrase is very relevant where academic success is concerned.

As a student you must spend quality time every single day reviewing and looking over your class material. "Why?" It causes you to better understand it.

Spend time reviewing your class subjects every single day, not just when you have the class on that day.

When I was a sophomore student attending Norfolk State University I carried 16 credits worth of classes. I had a three credit Chemistry course where I had classes scheduled on Monday, Wednesday, and Friday.

Not only did I study for this course before and after class on those days, but I spent time studying the material on Tuesday, Thursdays and even the weekend. Even when I took easier classes like Physical Education, I would spend some time reviewing that subject as well every day; even if it meant running in place for 5 minutes or so.

When you look at your class material every day, it alleviates procrastination, and it opens doorways for you to be better equipped for class assignments and tests.

Also, by studying everyday you will begin to identify which subjects you need extra help in. You will know if you need to schedule office time with your professor or a teacher's assistant.

What you repeatedly do everyday becomes a habit. So make a habit of studying your class subjects for a good amount of time even when you don't have the class.

Use your Mouth to Increase your Academic Learning

It was third grade, and every single day before going to bed I would stand in front of my parents and say.

1 times 1 is 1.
1 times 2 is 2.
1 times 3 is 3.
8 times 3 is 24.
8 times 4 is 32.
12 times 9 is 108.
12 times 10 is 120.

Do you remember those? Multiplication Tables, right? (or some people call it "Times Tables").

The same way you learned the multiplication tables is the same way you can increase your present academic learnings. Your mouth is a powerful tool available to increase memorization.

Another great example of using your mouth for learning is verbalizing the lyrics to your favorite song.

"I believe I can fly....I believe I can touch the sky...I think about it every night and day...I spread my wings and fly away...I believe I can soar...I see me running through that opening doooorrrrrr.."

The way I learned R. Kelley's hit song is by listening to the song, thinking about the words of the song, pondering the lyrics over and over in my mind and repeatedly singing the song to myself, or out-loud (normally in the shower).

You too can increase your learnings of the subjects you face by REPEATEDLY:

1. Listening to your professor

2. Thinking about the content you read from books

3. Reviewing and pondering your notes

4. Using your mouth to quote, discuss, verbalize, or talk about your class subject out-loud.

Talking your way to memorization and understanding, is a sure way to an "A"!

That concludes Play #7.25. Developing key academic habits and taking action is your guarantee to academic success and improved grades

Game Time

Well this brings me to the end of Playing Your "A" Game and I hope that this book has made a major impact in your life and educational career. To help you remember what you've read, here is a list of the 'plays' we've covered.

Play#1 - Have a Pep Rally

Play#2 - Set Your Winner's Mindset

Play#3 - See School As Your Full-Time Job

Play#4 - See Your Bulls-eye and Hit It

Play#5 - Sharpen Your Focus

Play#6 - Get Your Game Up

Play#7 - Stop The Stress Test Mess

Play #7.25 - Set Your Habits and Leave Them There

Winners are not the ones that only show up for the game, but they are the ones that play their "A" Game.

Meet Kantis Simmons

ROCKET SCIENTIST RAISES STUDENTS
TO NEW ALTITUDES

Former NASA scientist Kantis Simmons is on a mission.

As the nation's leading academic success strategist, he's aiming to put an end to the academic failure epidemic sweeping across America's high schools and colleges.

And he's winning; the schools he works with see a 15% - 23% improvement in student performance and test scores.

Through his speeches and his resources, students, parents and educators are fired up by experiencing the passion and practicality of Mr. Simmons philosophy for themselves.

Students readily respond when Mr. Simmons shares his advice and proven strategies for success, because he has emphatically walked the walk.

"Certificates, diplomas and degrees are keys! They open the doors in your life" - Kantis Simmons

Overcoming the challenge of growing up with a birth defect (7.25 fingers) on his left hand, Mr. Simmons now has 3 degrees.

With a Bachelor of Science degree in Chemistry from Norfolk State University, a Master of Science degree in Textile and Fiber Engineering from Georgia Tech, and a Master of Science degree in Polymer Science from Lehigh University his career includes developing new products for Mobil Chemical Company, creating new contact lenses for CIBA Vision, and improving military air crafts for NASA.

Hundreds of thousands of students have already been inspired by Mr. Simmons speaking; to get better grades, improve on standardized tests, stay enrolled in school and succeed in life.

As the author of 5 books, he and has been featured on NBC, Time Warner's Peachtree TV, and Radio One.

Educators agree "Kantis Simmons provides more than motivational rhetoric and theory. He gives real life solutions that bring real-life results! He is the real deal."

If you would like to hear his story and have you students, parents and educators experience his excitement and strategies please invite him to your next event by visiting:

www.KantisSimmons.com

180

"If you want your audience to be motivated and inspired to exceed their potential, then do yourself a huge favor and book my friend Kantis Simmons to speak at your next event. Your audience will love his message as it will empower every person to achieve their goals. And his book, Playing Your 'A' Game, is a must read for all students!"

- James Malinchak
Co-Author, Chicken Soup for the College Soul
Co-Author, Chicken Soup for the Athlete's Soul
"Two-Time College Speaker of the Year!"

"Kantis Simmons provides more than motivational rhetoric and theory. He givesreal life solutions that bring real-life results! He's the real deal and your audience will remember his message for a real long time!"

- Jonathan Sprinkles
Connection Coach, TV Personality
Author, "You Were Born an Original
Author, "Get Off Your But & Make It Hppen"

"I have never heard a success system quite like this one. Kantis Simmons' powerful 7.25 system will elevate your students thinking and academic status."

- Professor Joe Martin
Speaker, Author, Professor, Consultant
Author, "Tricks of the Grade"
Author, "Good Teachers Never Quit"

"When it comes to speaking about Academic Success and Overcoming Adversity, Kantis is one speaker that I highly endorse to the schools and parents I work with."

- Josh Shipp
Teen Behavior Expert & TV Host of Jump Shipp
Author, "Teen's Guide to World Domination

Hear What Educators Say About
Kantis Simmons' Speaking Programs

"Kantis Simmons presents Motivational information to help students plan for the future. Superb delivery of information. "
- Sylvia Adams, Guidance Counselor
Early County High School (Blakely, GA)

"Kantis Simmons was energetic and the information presented was outstanding. It reinforces what we are trying to let our freshman know. Once again a very beneficial program to kick off our school year for our freshman. All schools should contract with this program because it provides your freshman with the necessary information to be successful."
- Joe Fuline, Associate Principal
Struthers High School (Struthers, OH)

"Very positive, upbeat. I recommend the information that Kantis presents..It's current, helpful and provide valuable information to students. Mr. Simmons, was warm, friendly and immediately caught the students interest. "
- Rebecca Rye, Counselor
Forest Park High School (Forest Park, GA)

Mr. Simmons talk was great in engaging the students in the thinking process about goal setting and higher learning. Kantis Simmons is a dynamic speaker. Keep this program going. It was extremely useful for urban student. It was just GREAT!
- Annie Aaron, Curriculum Director,
Denby Tech & Prep School (Detroit, MI)

"Audience participation and the energy from Kantis was wonderful; however the target and the test taking strategies were great program points. This presentation was very engaging and relevant to the issues facing high school students today. The content and the delivery were appropriate and on point. I cannot think of anything that would improve the program at this time."
- Charlene Hampton, Guidance Counselor
Crisp Co High School (Cordele, GA)

"Kantis Simmons was obviously comfortable with students and engaged students in meaningful dialogue. He presented an excellent program. It goes hand in glove with information counselors are providing to our students. We bring him back again and again."
- Rodger Hudson, Guidance Counselor
Monroe Area High School (Monroe, GA)

"His energy and content - reinforces our message to students."
- Suzanne Bobalik, Principal
Carman-Ainsworth High School (Flint, MI)

"Kantis Simmons was TOP NOTCH. He knows what to say and how to interact with the students. Kantis Simmons did an outstanding job."
- Janice Cumbelander, Guidance Counselor
Greenville High School, (Greenville,GA)

"Kantis Simmons has the distinguishing presence of a man who commands any room, captivates his audience and has an award winning personality to watch. His lecture was a hit with our audience. He's the expert!"
- Angelyne Butler, Asst. TRIO Director
Georgia Perimeter College, (Clarkston, GA)

Hear What Students Say About
Kantis Simmons' Speaking Programs

"As a mother, wife and student, your system has not only helped me in School, but in everything I do. I hear your phrase of Play Your 'A' Game ringing in my conscious. Because of your 7.25 system Kantis, I will finally be graduating from college - and with good grades."
- Mechelle Wallace, Delta State University

"The statement that you made about the professors only professing the assignment and it was the students responsibility to understand and also learn what they need to know in college has stuck with me and has helped a lot of the students that we mentor."
- Antoinette Sibley, Education Counselor

"Kantis' talk took me from a "C" student to a 4.0 freshman, but his 7.25 System made me a better all-around person. And now a graduate."
-William Powell, Morehouse College, Atlanta, GA

"I had to pick a speech to go to for one of my classes and randomly I chose yours. I'm definitely glad I did. I thought that it would be another boring presentation I had to sit through, but that was the most fun I've had where I've had to listen to a motivational speaker. The fact that you involved the audience the entire time, you didn't just preach to us and the passion you had while in front of us definitely made it worth my time."
- Camille Marie Chirillo, Radford University, Radord, VA

"Your speech was awesome and it equipped me to pass my semester with a 4.0."
- John Gary, Savannah State University, Savannah, GA

Additional Notes

Additional Notes

Additional Notes

Additional Notes

9 780976 781219